W9-AEE-619

AFRICAN NATIONALISM
IN THE TWENTIETH CENTURY

HANS KOHN

Professor Emeritus of History
The City College of New York

AND

WALLACE SOKOLSKY

New York University

AN ANVIL ORIGINAL
under the general editorship of
LOUIS L. SNYDER

D. VAN NOSTRAND COMPANY, INC.

PRINCETON, NEW JERSEY

TORONTO   LONDON

NEW YORK

TO
THOSE WHO
STRIVE FOR UNDERSTANDING
AMONG ALL PEOPLE

D. VAN NOSTRAND COMPANY, INC.
120 Alexander St., Princeton, New Jersey (*Principal office*); 24 West 40 St., New York, N.Y.
D. VAN NOSTRAND COMPANY (Canada), LTD.
25 Hollinger Rd., Toronto 16, Canada
D. VAN NOSTRAND COMPANY, LTD.
358, Kensington High Street, London, W.14, England

PRINTED IN THE UNITED STATES OF AMERICA

PREFACE

This book attempts to deal with one phase of the African kaleidoscope, nationalism. Though all nationalisms are unique, they have much in common. With this in mind, we have sought to trace African nationalism through some of its manifestations, changes, and nuances. We have tried to be suggestive rather than exhaustive, providing an introduction to the further study of a fascinating aspect of this turbulent twentieth century.

Our warmest thanks are due to Miss Shirley Hochberg and Miss Dorothea Crandall, who helped to type the manuscript, and above all to Professor Louis L. Snyder, the Editor of the Anvil Series, for his friendship and guidance.

HANS KOHN
WALLACE SOKOLSKY

New York City

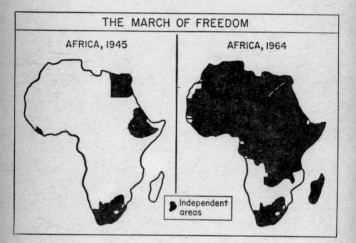

THE MARCH OF FREEDOM

AFRICA, 1945

AFRICA, 1964

Independent
areas

TABLE OF CONTENTS

Part 1

AFRICAN NATIONALISM

— 1 —

INTRODUCTION

African nationalism is an undeniable force in today's world. A generation ago, however, Lord Hailey's massive *An African Survey* (1938), absorbed as it was with the problems of administration, barely alluded to it. And as late as 1947 Obafemi Awolowo in his *Path to Nigerian Freedom,* while affirming that the Hausa, Ibo, and Yoruba were nations, denied that Nigeria constituted one. By contrast, in the year of Nigeria's independence, 1960, Sam Epelle's *The Promise of Nigeria* asserted that all who live in Nigeria realize that they have one future and that the differences among them are not sufficiently deep-rooted to break the country into warring parts. At the first institute on contemporary Africa held in the United States at Northwestern University in 1951 a high-ranking Belgian colonial official stated that he thought Belgium would remain in the Congo for another seventy-five years. During 1960, seventeen African countries, the Belgian Congo included, became independent.

Yet, the speed with which African states attained political independence should not have occasioned excessive surprise, for the march of anti-imperialism and nationalism after World War II in Asia and the Arab world was there for all to see. Certainly Africans saw it, were stimulated by it, and acted upon it. (*See Reading No. 1.*) There had been, to be sure, a sentiment of African nationalism before its acceleration during the war as newspapers and parties agitated for self-government. And one could say of the pre-war period, depending upon one's definition of the term, that in some areas residual "nationalism" (what many would term tribalism) existed. These pressures for independence, nevertheless, were minor in comparison with the flood-tide of nationalist interest, organization, activity, and success since

8

1945. Although it once was dismissed as a pastime of the intellectual elite, and the former Governor-General of Nigeria, Lord Milverton, in an address before the Royal African Society in 1956 said that African nationalism is "very often . . . just the craving for power by a small group of individuals," African nationalism has sunk deep roots. Dozens of political parties throughout Africa contain "national" in their titles (*see Reading No. 2*), and if the prime ingredient of nationalism is the *will to be a nation,* despite boundary disputes, internal friction, and the instability of regimes—conditions by no means exclusively African—then African nationalism is a growing reality. Tom Mboya, General Secretary of the Kenya African National Union, calls it "the dominant social and political force in contemporary Africa."

Ironically, nationalism has arisen at a time when many intellectuals are surfeited with its excesses, look upon it as an anachronism, and are seeking wider political entities. Nationalism, though, in and of itself, is neither good nor bad. In the minds of African leaders, it is no longer thought of in anti-imperialist terms, its original prime motivation. Nationalism is now conceived of as the necessary framework for and propelling force behind catapulting Africa into a complex, industrial world. African leaders rarely seek to return to a pre-European status. They are primarily forward-looking, and while anxious to preserve their culture, also want the best of modern industrial society. Wanting it, of course, and securing it must be bridged by hard thinking, hard working, belt-tightening, and concerted effort. As Kwame Nkrumah has noted in his autobiography *Ghana* (1959), "The economic independence that should follow and maintain political independence demands every effort from the people, a total mobilisation of brain and man power resources." Tanganyika's President Julius Nyerere refers not merely to *uhuru* but *uhuru na kazi*—freedom and work. *Consequently, the new role for African nationalism is to harness the future.* But economic charts have less drama than fighting for freedom. Five-year plans may be less soul-demanding and psychologically less immediately rewarding than demonstrations for liberty. African nationalism's problem, then, is to provide enough circuses while striving for more bread. If Africans become impatient with the long economic pull, or if their leadership becomes tainted by corruption or arrogance, confusion will be compounded. During a transition which may be quite long and troublesome, *nationalism, either local, regional, or continent-wide,* may be the cement to hold society together. African nationalism not only is here but, on whatever level, is here to stay.

Janheinz Jahn in his recent *Muntu: The New African Culture* (1961) states: "Neo-African culture clearly demonstrates that culture is not biologically inherited, that . . . customs and capabilities, thoughts and judgments are not innate." Cultural variations and nationalism do not rest upon biological differences. If there is nothing sacred about a particular culture, and national self-determination *per se* is not necessarily a political ultimate, one may yet sympathize with the movements for political and cultural independence. As others demand it for themselves, Africans can rationalize their wish for controlling their destinies with as much (or little) justification as the French, Portuguese, Belgians, or British. Africans may not be any more virtuous than Europeans, but they "prefer self-government with danger to servitude in tranquillity."

The "granting" of independence to many African states, while it had elements of the spirit of "trusteeship" in it, was due basically to *pressure* exerted upon the colonial powers. African nationalism, then, as nationalism elsewhere, emerged with a measure of truculence. (*See Reading No. 3.*) Being young, it is not without idealism.

A main point in Lord Hemingford's brief *Nationalism in Africa* (1954) is that talking about Africa as a whole is both feasible and necessary. Two noted anthropologists, Herskovits and Bascom, have recently called for appropriate caution. "There is no African culture which has not been affected in some way by European contact, and there is none which has entirely given way before it. . . ." It is to be hoped that sophisticated readers will make their own qualifications for many sweeping statements.

Characteristics of African Nationalism. Modern African nationalism is the product of European stimuli.

Ndabaningi Sithole, author of *African Nationalism* (1959), has observed that the African had to be *detribalized* before he could aspire nationally. And the Report of the Seminar on Racialism held at Kampala in 1961 says that African societies originally were formed on the basis of linguistic, clan, and tribal affinity and "that in this form African societies were not nations as such." Diedrich Westermann in *The African Today and Tomorrow* (1939) believes that true national states were the exception, and Maurice Delafosse in *The Negroes of Africa* (1931) says that what predominated was the little kingdom "whose unity is of geographic rather than ethnic order." On the other hand, a case can be made for the view that the Ewe, Kikuyu, Baganda, Yoruba, Barotse, Zulus, and others existed as "nations" prior to European contact. Jomo Kenyatta, legendary nationalist of Kenya, has written in *Facing Mount Kenya* (1938) that the Gikuyu (Kikuyu) possessed a "spirit of collectivism and national solidarity which they have been able to maintain from time immemorial." Obviously, the problem is a semantic one. In seeking the roots of African nationalism one may find evidence to support both positions. Paradoxical though it may appear, traditionalists and modernizers, although often having excoriated each other, have also reinforced the drive toward self-government. Thomas Hodgin has observed in his *African Political Parties* (1961) that the structure, programs, and ideologies of some African parties have to be understood in their relations with *pre*-colonial political systems, e.g., the Northern People's Congress in the Northern Region of Nigeria. But other "peoples," as he terms them, such as the Yoruba, Ewe, and Kikuyu, are generally led by "westerners." Even as the modernizers have despised certain traditional practices, they have taken pride in the achievements and heroes of the past. R. L. Buell's two-volume *The Native Problem in Africa* (1928) quotes the Reverend S. R. B. Attoh Ahuma, writing in 1911, to the effect that "We are a nation. We have a past. We own a concentric system of government; of one Race born and bred upon our soil. With the Akan language one can cover a seaboard 350 miles in extent" (*The Gold Coast Nation and National Conscience*). The association of "nation" with earlier institutions may be seen in the retention of *separate* tribal groupings in some urban areas. Links with the past exist on many levels.

The direction for most of Africa, however, is to be found in allegiance to the new states whose limits rarely correspond to tribal boundaries. Elspeth Huxley may continue to see Africa in tribal terms, and assuredly these ties are strong, but W. M. Macmillan in *Africa Emergent* (1949) calls the Westernizers the "gear-moving factor in modern Africa. They are in closer touch with the masses than it is the fashion to suppose." Sithole agrees that the majority of Africans continue to live in "their primitive stage. . . . But in all revolutions it is the minority that counts." After surveying the story of vanished civilizations in *African Glory* (1954), J. C. de Graft Johnson is of the same opinion: ". . . Negroes are attempting to achieve in a single generation what it took others centuries to achieve. . . . The process of assimilation and adaptation may not be complete, but the forward movement is unmistakable. . . ." Cultural and social memories linger, but a new nationalism has been and is being forged. New boundaries, new political forms, new economic relationships, and a new intellectual outlook are modifying the old Africa. The sense of fuller participation in government is felt by the detribalized African in that he no longer is a colonial "subject" or a cog in a tribal wheel rendered innocuous by colonial supervision. He is now, as during the French Revolution, a "citizen." The process, obviously, is far from complete. Whether through conviction or due to a frank concession to popular conservatism, African leaders have resurrected the glories of old. The medieval kingdoms of Mandingo, Ghana, Songhay, Melli, nineteenth-century heroes such as the Basuto chief, Moshesh, the Zulu conqueror, Chaka, Bishop Crowther, and such commemorative events as the Fanti confederation of 1871 enhance current national pride. The result, nevertheless, is that earlier tribal or "national" successes have become part of the modern national, mythic past. A Nigerian, F. Oladipo Onipede, in an article on "African Nationalism" says that younger nationalist leaders in order to appeal to the illiterate masses have had to give African symbols and institutions priority over the ideas and language of Western liberalism. A subtle symbiosis, at times sincere, at times pragmatically utilized, has joined the traditional and modern sense of community.

The conditions leading to detribalization and nationalism are well-known—the disruption of the traditional agricultural economy; the luring of labor to plantations, mines, and factories by taxation, force, and persuasion; missionary schools which taught the dignity of all men before God; secular liberalism; the traveling of Africans abroad as students, laborers, and soldiers; new European boundaries that cut across old tribal divisions; improved transportation and communications facilities; European *lingua francas;* the example of Asian revolt—all these fostered the spirit of nationalism. But above all, European racial arrogance, either overt or patronizing, bred bitter resentment. (*See Reading No. 4.*) In *The Challenge of Africa* (1962) a former leader of the opposition in Ghana, Professor K. A. Busia, declares, "The fact that African nationalism is, in the first place, a demand for racial equality is its most conspicuous attribute." Sithole remarks succinctly, "African nationalism is a struggle against white supremacy." Africans sought freedom and control of government in their own lands. To achieve it they *re*-united under the banner of nationalism.

— 2 —

AFRICA AND WORLD HISTORY

Comparative Nationalisms. The 1950's were characterized by a new phenomenon which continued into the 1960's, the participation of Africa as an active partner in world history. Of the great continents, Africa alone, from the European perspective, had been strangely passive and silent through the ages. This, of course, had not been true of North Africa. There, in Egypt, existed the seat of one of the oldest civilizations and imperial powers of mankind. There, Islam quickly spread from western Asia and made lasting contributions to the intellectual life of the Mediterranean. But Africa south of the Sahara remained unknown until the age of exploration of the late fifteenth century. These explorations were confined to the coasts, where a few European settlements were established. Inland Africa, however, was only explored in the middle of the nineteenth century, and the partition of Africa among the colonial powers took place only in the 1880's. The integration of Africa south of the Sahara into the political organization of the known parts of the globe started scarcely more than 80 years ago. Even in 1950 few believed that out of this so recent passive integration the African people would soon emerge as active political partners in history. They have done it under the flag of nationalism.

The process is not new. It happened in the middle of the nineteenth century in central Europe and in the beginning of the twentieth century in eastern Europe. It has happened in the middle of the twentieth century, with astonishing speed, in Asia. But though the end of the colonial empires in Asia and North Africa after World War II came as a surprise to many observers, the rise of nationalism in the Middle East, in Asia and the Far East had been unmistakably going on for decades. Its awakening in Egypt can be dated back at least to 1879, when the first popular military regime under Colonel Ahmed Arabi tried to overthrow the corrupt court aristocracy and to put an end to foreign interference. The Indian National Congress was established in 1885, and from that date an unbroken though changing line has led to Jawaharlal Nehru. The transformation of Japan into a modern nation began in the 1870's, and in 1911 the Chinese revolution started that country's struggle against domestic corruption and autocracy and against foreign encroachments. The triumphant self-assertion of nationalism in Asia and North Africa after the end of World War II could thus point to a preceding preparatory history of almost a century. Little was known of similar movements in Africa. The people of the Congo or Angola seemed even in 1950 submissively to accept their passive role. Yet, at the beginning of the 1960's a new nationalism was asserting itself all over Africa.

Nationalism has been a modern phenomenon even among the peoples of central, eastern, and southern Europe. It has come to Africa only very recently. Africa is the last continent to enter the age of nationalism and thereby the modern age. The manifestations of nationalism differ widely according to the historical circumstances of its rise, to the cultural traditions and the social structure of the peoples involved. Yet with all due difference, the state of mind which manifests itself in nationalism is similar everywhere, in Europe and in Asia, in Africa and in Latin America. In the age of nationalism peoples wish no longer to be objects of history made by others, but wish to feel themselves active agents of their own history. They no longer accept their traditional position as unchangeable. They wish to improve their position in their own land and to improve the position of their country in relation to other countries.

This search for a new status demands an adjustment of existing social and psychological attitudes. Such an adjustment takes time and produces critical tensions. The peoples of Europe, Asia, and the Americas have often passed through long upheavals, bitter controversies and struggles before they became integrated nations. Seen in perspective, the transition from traditional to modern national society in Africa has not only been rapid, but relatively smooth. The events which started in Africa in the 1950's represent the last stage in the world-wide revolutionary transformation of society, a transformation which got under way in seventeenth and eighteenth century northwest Europe and North America and has spread with accelerating speed in the following two centuries until it has by now become world-wide. In this transformation which is fundamentally one and the same everywhere, the unity of mankind, long postulated by universal religions, by the Stoics, by the rational humanism of the age of Enlightenment, is for the first time becoming a reality. The rise of nationalism, the quest for equality and human dignity, which now transform ancient and primitive tribal societies in sub-Saharan Africa, put the capstone to the growing edifice of humanity. We are at the beginning of a new era of history, in which all formerly isolated and secluded parts of the globe are entering into communication and intercourse on a footing of legal equality.

Diversity of Interests.   At present Africans not only are entering into contact with the outside world as recognized partners, they are meeting each other for the first time. Until very recently, distances, lack of communication, and absence of a common language, prevented their coming together. Now, an African consciousness is growing. This common consciousness does not necessarily imply unification or unity, any more than it does in Europe or Latin America. From region to region, interests differ and conflict. Some African frontiers will be hotly disputed among African states. The relationships of Somalia and of Mauritania to their neighbors is uneasy, and there will be more such cases, just as there have been and are bitter frontier disputes among European and Latin American nations. Well-established élites have their vested interests in state boundaries and power and do not wish to cede their place to competitors for Pan-African or regional leadership. Efforts to federate have so far failed. But they failed equally among Scandinavian or Central American states, though these show an infinitely greater affinity among themselves than do the various African regions. A Pan-African unity or even regional unity may not be expected in any foreseeable future. Problems, though fundamentally similar, differ nevertheless very much in the various parts of the continent south of the Sahara. Tribal traditions and customs, languages and religions show an amazing variety. Only in the north, from Morocco to Egypt, do there exist past traditions of unity which possibly could point to closer cooperation in the future. Memories of a great common history and the powerful realities of a common language, culture, and religion support a feeling of belonging together. But these elements are not confined to Arab-speaking Africa. They reach across the Sinai peninsula to the lands of the Fertile Crescent and the Arab peninsula. In this linguistic-cultural community Egypt occupies—by geography, population, history, economic wealth, and cultural achievements—a central position. It links Africa to Asia, and Europe to the world east of the Suez Canal. Arabism and Islam, however, are not confined to the southern shore of the Mediterranean. They penetrate far into Africa, in the Sudan, in Somalia and Nigeria. Islamic influence, centered in the ancient traditional and in the large modern schools of Egypt, is making progress throughout middle Africa.

Non-Alignment. Though they have close historical ties with the West and though most of their students and intellectuals study or have studied in the West, most Africans wish to maintain a policy of positive neutrality. Such a policy was probably best defined by the Prime Minister of Tanganyika, a British colony then in the last stage of its orderly transition to full independence. Julius Nyerere, knowns as a moderate, declared on June 1, 1961, in the National Assembly: "It would be wrong to describe independent Tanganyika's policy as that of neutralism, for the word neutral often carries a connotation of not caring. We do care, passionately, about the development of justice, of well being, and of peace throughout the world. We do care about the rights of man, about the independence and self-determination of nations or groups of nations. We do care about having peace both in Africa and in other parts of the world. On these great issues we cannot be neutral. But although our policy will not be one of passive neutrality, it will be independent."

The rise of nationalism in Africa came at a fateful moment in world history, though the Africans carry no responsibility for it. As a result of the two great twentieth-century wars, the Union of Socialist Soviet Republics and the United States of America emerged as the two strongest powers on earth. Representing opposite political traditions and philosophies of history and society, they entered into a competition which affected all the peoples of the earth. This competition between the democratic West and the communist East aggravated yet at the same time facilitated the rise of the new nations in Africa and Asia and the rapid march toward equality of Asians, Africans, and Latin Americans. Most Arabs and Africans know that they owe their education in the ideas of individual liberty, human equality, and social responsibility to the West. But they have witnessed, too, how much the West sinned by hypocrisy and disregard of its own principles. The newly awakened nations of Asia, Africa, and Latin America—awakened by the dynamic civilization of the modern West and its message of human rights—do not wish to be directly involved in the struggle between East and West. Domestic poverty, not outside communist aggression, seems to them the chief threat to their progress. They are not isolationists. They put their chief hope in the United Nations. Measures to strengthen the United Nations find their support. But they wish to be masters in their own house as much as other nations do, and not junior partners of great powers. They do not trust the latter's wisdom implicitly. After all, the two world wars were sparked in Europe, and the horrors of communism and fascism did not originate among colored peoples. Their judgment may sometimes be colored by anti-colonial resentment, but this resentment is not racial; it is hardly stronger than anti-British feeling has been among the Irish or anti-Austrian feeling among the Czechs.

Continuity vs. Innovation.   The rise of nationalism everywhere involved an emphasis on being oneself, on tradition and distinctiveness. But progress always, and especially in modern times, demands a break with ancient and restrictive traditions, with the immobilities and authority of caste, tribe, and extended family in favor of individuality, social mobility, and greater equality. The problem of the desirable relationship between continuity and innovation, though a universal problem, is of crucial urgency in the modernization of traditional society. Peter I and Lenin in Russia, Robespierre in France, Atatürk in Turkey tried to solve it radically in favor of innovation. But the traditional forms of life showed their continuous efficacy; 40 years after Atatürk's forceful secularization of Turkey, the events of 1960 revealed how strongly the villages and the smaller towns remained attached to traditional Islam. The future of evolving societies depends much more than do established modern societies upon the quality of leadership. This leadership may not always be democratic in the Western sense of representative government. Representative government as it exists in the English-speaking lands and in a few northern European countries has not shown consistent promise even in the Latin countries of Europe and America or in central-eastern Europe. It works in India where the ruling elite has been trained for more than a century in the English political system. But elsewhere, whether it be in Turkey or in Egypt, parliamentary regimes tended to strengthen the monopoly of the ruling group and were not effective in rooting out traditional corruption. There, as in other more advanced nations which disposed of military establishments, the military showed themselves as the one group which at least had the rudiments of modern efficiency, the discipline of team work, the sense of responsibility for the nation as a whole. In Europe and Latin America, the officers often stood for the vested interests of the ruling class. In Asia and Africa the officer personnel, largely drawn from the rising lower classes, were seriously concerned with improving the lot of the masses and carrying through the needed social and economic reforms in order to assure national survival in modern times. In most of Africa, however, no native officer corps existed. As a result the same role was played by civilian leaders.

Leadership. These leaders are supported by their peoples. In the elections held under British supervision in Kenya at the end of February 1961, Tom Mboya, a leader of the Kenya African National Union, emerged as victor in an election which a Reuters dispatch described as one in which the new African voters belied European fears of violence and displayed good humor throughout. Though Mboya was elected with a great majority, he declared on March 10 that "in the initial stages" a one-party government would be "necessary" for stability and for the development of democracy in Kenya. "Danger would come not from traditions or tribalism, but from a struggle for power between the parties. Inevitably this would produce violence and instability." Similar views are held in Ghana and elsewhere in Africa. Like Nasser's Egypt, Bourguiba's Tunisia represents a social as well as a political revolution, in which national unity and solidarity gain at the expense of debate and discussion. Most Tunisians feel that strong opposition movements "would only breed chaos and demagoguery and that the one-party political system may be the only hope for the development of democratic traditions in Africa." Nasser's government, perhaps less monolithic but not more democratic in the Anglo-American sense than Bourguiba's, is

the least corrupt and the most popular government Egypt
ever had, giving the people a feeling of participation, of
dignity, of being respected and cared for.

African leadership is young. Dr. Hastings K. Banda,
the popular leader of Nyasaland's Malawi Congress Party,
in 1961 announced the party's candidates for the first
democratic elections in the territory. They include most
of his principal lieutenants with an average age of about
twenty. There is today a feeling of hope throughout
Africa unknown a very few years ago. In many places the
transition has been smooth, though not everywhere as
smooth as it was in some of the British West African territories, beginning with Ghana in March 1957. The
tenacity of colonialism has made or is making the transition difficult and cruel in Kenya, Algeria, Guinea, in the
Congo and in Angola, in "Rhodesia" and in the Union
of South Africa. But the wind of change, of which Prime
Minister Harold Macmillan spoke so eloquently in South
Africa, is blowing everywhere, and not only in Africa.

It would be incorrect to consider the African problem
fundamentally different from that of Asia, Latin America,
or the underdeveloped parts of Europe like Spain or
Sicily. Local differences exist everywhere, but the fundamental problem of the adaptation of traditional or
medieval societies to modern civilization is the same.
Everywhere, following the example of the modern West,
the underprivileged, the disinherited, the have-nots aspire
to equality. Their rise, necessarily, involves the curtail-
ment of the privileges of the former privileged. The
tensions and discontents created by this process are
utilized by communism for its own purposes. But communism did not create the tensions. The example of the
West did, and its modern history has been the story of
the emancipation of underprivileged classes and groups.
Some observers feel that the modern West could commit
no greater error than to make itself the defender of the
status quo and to attribute the changes going on to the
influence or plots of communism.

Some Western representatives have at times used
language which seemed to express a racial or cultural superiority complex or a "realistic" *Machtpolitik* of alleged
strategic interests. To others such language and the under-

lying sentiment runs counter to the spirit of modern civilization and undermines its ethos. The revolution of the third quarter of the twentieth century, in which Africa forms one of the pivotal points, challenges the West—above all the two great nations in which democracy rests on solid foundations, Britain and the United States—to understand the historical forces at work, their origin and nature, and not to sacrifice the realization of its own values and its own future to the alleged and shifting needs of a current power struggle.

— 3 —

AMERICAN INFLUENCES ON AFRICAN NATIONALISM BEFORE WORLD WAR II

Impetus from America. African nationalism received much of its initial impetus from America. That the catalyst for Pan-Africanism and African nationalism came from abroad is not surprising. Sun Yat-sen, De Valera, Garibaldi, Gandhi, and others spent much of their time overseas. Though William E. B. Du Bois, founder of the National Association for the Advancement of Colored People and left-wing scholar, is generally credited with having been the "father" of Pan-Africanism, others, too, played significant roles in creating an interest in the "African personality" and African freedom. Several West Indians contributed to the triangular influence on America and Africa. Indicative of the American interest in Africa before World War I is the impact that American Negro churches had on those in South Africa and Nigeria at the turn of the century and the Gold Coast's modification of its immigration regulations in order to keep out "undesirable Negro Americans." Though the earlier "Back to Africa" movement as represented by the Liberian example was opposed after the Civil War by Negro leaders, Edward Blyden, "pioneer theorist of the 'African personality,'" declared in 1883, "No people

can interpret Africans but Africans," and Dr. Martin R.
Delaney, a nineteenth-century physician, also spoke of
"Africa for the African."

Prior to World War I, concern with Negro history in
the United States spread rapidly as part of a general
cultural renaissance. (*See Reading No. 5.*) Carter G.
Woodson, founder of the *Journal of Negro History,* was
pre-eminent in this absorption in the African background,
his *The African Background Outlined* being a symbol
of the aroused interest. An incipient attitude of *negritude*
may be found in Woodson's comment on the "Negro's
philosophy of life." ". . . Some of these ideas, of course,
would seem very much like the principles advanced by
centers of thought outside of Africa, but in certain respects
they show characteristics peculiar to that continent or
to those people. We are undoubtedly justified in thinking of the African as having a philosophy of his own.
. . ." It is significant that the pride taken in past achievements should range over the Continent—from ancient
Ethiopia and Egypt to the West African medieval kingdoms of Kumbi (Ghana), Manding (Melle), Songhay,
Mossi, and Hausa. Boundaries blurred from the distance
of thousands of miles. Along similar lines, Nkrumah was
to help organize the African Students' Association of
America and Canada, an expression of the *Pan-*Africanist
influence from America. The very fact that Africans increasingly came to America to study was to leave its
mark upon African nationalism. From Chilembwe of
Nyasaland and Aggrey of the Gold Coast the trans-
Atlantic stimulus spread through such modern leaders as
Azikiwe, Banda, and Nkrumah.

Garveyism. Flashing dramatically through this
growing interest in Africa came the remarkable Garvey
movement. As Edmund Cronen, his biographer in *Black
Moses* (1955), phrases it, Marcus Garvey's ". . . peculiar
gift of oratory, a combination of bombast and stirring
heroics, awakened fires of Negro nationalism. . . . He
told his listeners . . . that a black skin was not a badge
of shame but rather a glorious symbol of national greatness. He promised a Negro nation in the African home-
land. . . ." Born in Jamaica in 1887, Garvey was a
Negro of Koromantee stock; this was a "fact of tre-
mendous importance," Padmore states in *Pan-Africanism*

or Communism (1956). Irritated by what he considered
to be the annoying superciliousness and discriminatory
actions of the Jamaican mulattoes, he stressed separation
of the black and white peoples and thereby obtained support from the Ku Klux Klan. While in London in 1912
he imbibed the nationalism of the Egyptian publisher of
the *African Times* and *Orient Review,* Duse Mohammed
Ali, and by 1920, his Universal Negro Improvement
Association (founded in Jamaica in 1914) blossomed in
New York. The *Negro World,* his newspaper, and numerous speeches proclaimed the motto of the U.N.I.A.:
"One God, One Aim, One Destiny." The objects of the
Association were:

> To establish a universal confraternity among the race; to
> promote the spirit of pride and love; to reclaim the fallen;
> to administer to and assist the needy; to assist in civilizing
> the backward tribes of Africa; to assist in the development
> of independent nations and communities; to establish a
> central nation for the race; to establish commissaries or
> agencies in the principal countries and cities of the world
> for the representation of all Negroes; to promote a con-
> scientious spiritual worship among the native tribes of
> Africa; to establish universities, colleges, academies and
> schools for the racial education and culture of the people;
> to work for better conditions among Negroes everywhere.

Master showman that he was, Garvey was elected
Provisional President of Africa at a U.N.I.A. meeting in
New York in 1920. (*See Reading No. 6.*) To back up
such slogans as "Africa for the Africans," "Renaissance
of the Black Race," and "Ethiopia Awake," a Universal
African Legion, the Universal Black Cross Nurses, the
Universal African Motor Corps and an ill-fated Black
Star Line were formed. Garvey made use of a Black
Christ and a Black Madonna in his African Orthodox
Church, continually exhorting his followers to display
pride in race. "We believe in the freedom of Africa for
the Negro people of the world . . . we also demand
Africa for the Africans at home and abroad." Despite
criticism, according to J. A. Rogers in *World's Great
Men of Color,* he was the "first and only black man who
ever succeeded in making Negroes pay for Negro agitation."

To implement his colonization plans, negotiations were

opened with the Liberian government, which soon became suspicious of what it thought were Garvey's ambitions, and little practical effect came from his plans for settlement. The colonial powers looked askance at his activities. J. A. Rogers, who knew him well, says: "His cause was just, too, but his methods were twisted, archaic, perverse. He undoubtedly wanted to help the downtrodden blacks but like every other autocrat believed that the end justifies the means. . . ." Padmore accuses him of lacking tact and diplomacy. Du Bois, who believed that Garveyism vitiated his own Pan-African efforts, says of it in his *The World and Africa* (1947): ". . . It represented a poorly conceived but intensely earnest determination to unite the Negroes of the world, especially in commercial enterprise. It used all the nationalist and racial paraphernalia of popular agitation, and its strength lay in its backing by the masses of West Indians and by increasing numbers of American Negroes. Its weakness lay in its demagogic leadership, poor finance, intemperate propaganda, and the natural apprehension it aroused among the colonial powers."

Although racial pride and African nationalism were cornerstones of his movement, Garvey never set foot on African soil. But Garvey's influence on Pan-Africanism, despite a jail sentence in 1925 for alleged fraud, and despite splits in the U.N.I.A., must be accounted considerable. Kwame Nkrumah writes: "But I think that of all the literature that I studied, the book that did more than any other to fire my enthusiasm was *Philosophy and Opinions of Marcus Garvey* published in 1923. Garvey with his philosophy of 'Africa for the Africans' and his 'Back to Africa' movement, did much to inspire the Negroes of America in the 1920s." Cronen cites the Kingston *Daily Gleaner* as crediting Garvey with personally converting Jomo Kenyatta to the philosophy of Africa for the Africans. As recently as October 1962 in an article in *The Negro History Bulletin* two authors write: "Garvey's works are divine and cannot be destroyed by man. Garvey was prepared and sent to his people by the same method that Moses, Christ, Confucius and Mohammed were sent to their people. Garvey most certainly is nonetheless greater than either of the four Saviours mentioned above."

Garvey's Black Zionism never appealed to American Negroes sufficiently to support a back-to-Africa migration, but his spirit lives on these days in a proliferation of Afro-American nationalist organizations. At a mass meeting in New York, June 10, 1961, sponsored by the African Colonization Society, handbills proclaimed that "Garvey was the greatest figure of the 20th century. Let's carry on his programme by uniting around his principle 'Africa for the Africans at home and abroad.'" The African Nationalist Pioneer Movement in an advertisement in the New York journal *African Opinion* exhorted all to "Join with us on the 17th of August 1961 (Garvey's birthday) . . . the spirit of Garveyism is on the march. . . . Let it be to all Africans everywhere, what March 17th means to the Irish. . . . We agree with Marcus Garvey's doctrine and programme, and are convinced that the Black Race is just as good if not better than any other race. . . ." And the United African Nationalist Movement with headquarters in New York, at the top of its list of aims, calls for "Africa for the Africans—Those at Home and Those Abroad." While Africa may not appeal to Afro-Americans in terms of mass emigration, in numerous, amorphous ways Africa in being free, may enhance their status in America. Summarizing the stimulus from America, a Nigerian who taught political science at Brown University, Dr. Essien-Udom, writes: "They were the vanguard of modern African nationalism, of the philosophers of 'Negritude,' of Pan-Africanism, and of Africa's rise to self-assertion in the contemporary world."

The First Pan-African Congresses. In a manner different from that of Garveyism but with overlapping goals, the activities of William E. B. Du Bois were to spark a series of Pan-African congresses of immeasurable importance in sustaining the concept of Pan-Africanism until its post-World War II maturation. Indeed, he has been called the "father" of Pan-Africanism. Although a congress of 1900 * had been largely ignored, Du Bois, American professor, writer, and founder of the

---

* The first "Pan-African" meeting (1900) organized by H. Sylvester Williams, a West Indian barrister, in London, protested the treatment of Africans in South Africa and Rhodesia but attracted little notice.

N.A.A.C.P., took it upon himself to have the voice of Africa expressed at the Versailles Peace Conference. Without credentials, he got no further than Colonel House, but with Clemenceau's private blessing (conscious of Senegalese help during the War), convened in 1919 in Paris what Padmore calls the first Pan-African Congress. (*See Reading No. 7.*) Fifty-seven delegates from fifteen countries attended, including twelve delegates from nine African countries. Special visas having been refused by the United States and colonial powers, attendance was limited. So, too, was the conference's effectiveness. The resolutions of the Congress, it might be noted, did *not* call for Pan-African *union,* but rather for *self-determination,* and this, too, "as fast as . . . development permits." That Du Bois did not believe in the likelihood of immediate results may be seen in his later observation, "My plans, as they developed, had in them nothing spectacular nor revolutionary. If in decades or a century, they resulted in such world organization of black men as would oppose a united front to European aggression, they certainly would not have been beyond my dream. But on the other hand, in practical reality, I knew the power and guns of Europe and America."

In 1921 Du Bois organized a second Pan-African Congress which met sequentially in London, Brussels, and Paris. Forty-one of the 113 delegates came from Africa, for the most part as individuals. In addition to repeating many of the ideas of the previous manifesto, the group demanded "Freedom in their own religion and social customs and with the right to be different and nonconformist." Although the second meeting as well as the first, stimulated a feeling of brotherhood amongst Africans and American Negroes, the ideas of Pan-Africanism were still largely confined to a small group of intellectuals. In fact, Du Bois acknowledges, even after the third Pan-African Congress, held in London and Lisbon, in 1923, that the Pan-African idea was still American rather than African. Du Bois' socialist orientation may well have had inserted the eighth demand: "The organization of commerce and industry so as to make the main objects of capital and labor the welfare of the many rather than the enriching of the few." The Fourth Pan-African Congress, held in New York in 1927, saw only a few African representatives, the Pan-African movement in the interim having lost ground. An abortive attempt to convene another meeting in 1929 fell by the boards as the French refused to sanction Tunis as a site, and the depression in the United States eliminated the funds of American Negro backers. As one observer has noted, Du Bois had ability, but little appeal for the Negro masses. Garvey was a poor organizer, but a dynamic and attractive personality. "A combination of the better qualities of the two might have led to real accomplishment." A more likely explanation for the "failure" of the conferences is that neither Pan-African sentiment nor conditions favorable to its realization had as yet crystalized.

A measure of frustration and futility was felt at the above meetings of the 1920's, but their very existence was important for the maintenance of a cadre of interested individuals ready to meet again when the time was propitious. Needless to say, the fact that the conferences had occurred, whatever their limitations, was to have value after World War II in providing a group with organizational knowledge, ready to lead anew. During the 1930's, the spirit of Pan-Africanism was kept from becoming dormant by the sense of Negro solidarity occasioned by Mussolini's attack on Ethiopia in 1935. Giving a measure of form to the feelings of anger and determination in these years was the International African Service Bureau established in 1937 in London. It was this Bureau that amassed the funds needed to convene the Fifth Pan-African Congress.

The Manchester Conference of 1945. The Fifth Pan-African Congress in 1945 was far more important than any of its predecessors. Again, Du Bois was a moving spirit, but this time, Africans themselves played a major role in its proceedings. Two hundred delegates met in Manchester, England, October 15-21; prominent among them were Dr. P. M. Milliard, T. R. Makonnen, George Padmore, Kwame Nkrumah, Peter Abrahams, and Jomo Kenyatta. In the congenial atmosphere of a Labour Party victory, hopes ran high for the attainment of independence. The left-orientation of the Congress may be gathered from the ending of a two-page article on the meeting, "The Congress in Perspective," written by Peter Abrahams, Publicity Secretary of the Pan-African Congress: *"Foward to the Socialist United States of Africa! Long Live Pan-Africanism!"* In the words of the conference rapporteur, Kwame Nkrumah, recently arrived after years in the United States: "Although this conference was the fifth of its kind that had taken place, it was quite distinct and different in tone, outlook and ideology from the four that had preceded it. While the four previous conferences were both promoted and supported mainly by middle-class intellectuals and bourgeois Negro reformists, this Fifth Pan-African Congress was attended by workers, trade unionists, farmers, co-operative societies and by African and other colored students. As a preponderance of members attending the Congress were African, its ideology became African nationalism— a revolt by African nationalism against colonialism, racialism and imperialism in Africa—and it adopted Marxist socialism as its philosophy. Like Garveyism, the first four conferences were not born of indigenous African consciousness. Garvey's ideology was concerned with *black* nationalism as opposed to *African* nationalism. And it was this Fifth Pan-African Congress that provided the outlet for African nationalism and brought about the awakening of African political consciousness. It became, in fact, a mass movement of Africa for the Africans."

Once again, only this time with greater assurance and determination, the demands of earlier congresses were affirmed. "Partnership," "trusteeship," "guardianship," and the "mandate system" were declared not to be in the interests of the people of West Africa. Indirect rule and pretentious constitutional reforms were condemned, the latter as "spurious." And the Congress observed: "That the artificial divisions and territorial boundaries created by the imperialistic powers are deliberate steps to obstruct the political unity of the West African peoples." The Congress also endorsed the call for self-government in East Africa and condemned South African racialism. Bringing its deliberations to a close, it asked the colonial powers to honor the Atlantic Charter, and ended its plea with, "We are determined to be free. . . . Therefore, we shall complain, appeal and arraign. We will make the world listen to the facts of our condition. We will fight in every way we can for freedom, democracy and social betterment."

In order to implement the Congress' proclamations, a Pan African Federation was set up in London with T. R. Makonnen as Secretary and editor of a new journal, *Pan-Africa*. Banned later from the colonies, it folded after acting as a clearing house for African affairs. By this time, however, the "positive action" called for at the Congress began to materialize. Aided by the world-wide surge of anti-imperialism, Pan-Africanism entered a new phase—the march toward freedom—freedom for *individual* African countries.

— 4 —

THE MARCH TO FREEDOM

Uhuru. "It is not in the British tradition to explore far-reaching constitutional issues until the force of circumstances makes it essential to do so." Thus, Lord Hailey in the first edition of his *An African Survey* (1938) calmly describes a policy which made African blood boil. Africans agreed that decolonization was always the result of pressure. Though the pressure gathered momentum after the Second World War, its antecedents merit description. "I travelled much in Africa between the wars, trekking widely, sometimes on foot or Model T truck, far away from centers and main roads. And yet I did not see any overt signs of discontent or antagonism." Thus writes Margery Perham, author of several noted books on Africa, in *The Colonial Reckoning* (1962). From another perspective, Oliver and Fage in their *A Short History of Africa* (1962) state that the appearance during this period of what some Europeans called "trousered blacks" and "handfuls of examination-bred students" was no less than "the most important event in African history."

Before the great divide, World War II, African nationalism was evidenced in a variety of ways: in political parties, in separatist churches, in a nationalist press, in strikes, in congresses abounding in manifestoes, in youth movements, and at times in violence. Most of the activity, in retrospect, was less substantive than symbolic of things to come, yet these precursors of nationalism cumulatively built up the psychology of rebellion, the habits of organizing for common purposes, leadership cadres and a "history" of nationalist activity. By comparison with what came after World War II, it is true that earlier nationalist ferment seems episodic, directed against specific grievances and lacking in coordination. Furthermore, at the time, it seemed largely to have failed. Yet, hindsight permits us to view this era, however abortive, as one of gestation leading later to more widespread national awareness and self-government. Many of the protest movements were not consciously nationalist in intent. Cumulatively, however, they did foster a sense of martyrdom, pride, bitterness, and in the case of the new youth, a determination to succeed where their elders had not. In addition to trans-Atlantic influences, there were extensive nationalist activities within Africa prior to 1945. These activities, on occasion, transcended borders. For example, Wallace Johnson of Sierra Leone and Nnamdi Azikwe of Nigeria were both expelled in the 1930's from the Gold Coast for their criticism of the government. And, of course, the National Congress of British West Africa (1920) had branches in the Gold Coast, Nigeria, Sierra Leone, and Gambia. Then too, Africans studying in England and France formed friendships that crossed parochial boundaries. Ladipo Solanke, who helped to organize the West African Students' Union in 1925, was the benevolent force behind a London African house that provided a haven for those students far from home. For the most part, however, agitation within Africa at this time was confined to territorial limits.

The countries to be described in the following pages have been selected because: Ghana was the initial leader in African nationalism and Pan-Africanism; Nigeria is Africa's largest country in population and illustrates the problems of federating diverse groups; and South Africa is the largest country south of the Sahara under a European-dominated government.

— 5 —

THE GOLD COAST TO GHANA: NKRUMAH SETS THE PACE

As he was leaving the United States in 1945 after ten years of study and hardship, and his ship passed the Statue of Liberty, Kwame Nkrumah through misty eyes vowed: "I shall never rest until I have carried your message to Africa." A dozen years later, as Prime Minister of the first African colony to gain freedom, Nkrumah, reflecting on the long and difficult road to self-government, again determined that "African nationalism was not [to be] confined to the Gold Coast—the new Ghana. From now on it must be Pan-African nationalism . . . and political emancipation must spread throughout the whole continent." Nkrumah's personality explains Ghana's leadership in the Pan-African drive. The explanation for Ghana's being the first colony to receive independence may be ascribed not only to his leadership, but to an extended history of struggle for African interests on the Gold Coast. As George Padmore has noted in *The Gold Coast Revolution* (1953), political consciousness among the masses may be quite recent, but "Gold Coast nationalism has deep roots and a long tradition."

The Bond of 1844. European concern with the West Coast of Africa goes back to the commercial revolution and the slave trade. After the abolition of the slave trade in the early nineteenth century, regular commerce continued, but on a modest scale. British governmental interest also was relatively small, although the dissolution in 1821 of the African Company of Merchants which had administered the coastal forts did not eliminate all British interest in the area. Coming to the aid of the coastal Fantis against the Ashantis in the interior in 1824 as they had in 1803, the British lost their Governor, Sir Charles McCarthy, whose skull thereafter was used as a drinking cup. Two years later the Ashantis were soundly defeated. By 1844, partly to curb the illicit slave trade, the British signed a Bond with the Fantis formally taking them under protection. But the Africans took "protection" literally rather than in terms of extensive colonial control. Twentieth-century nationalists view the Bond of 1844 as indicative of the autonomy of the tribes who had entered into the pact. Casely Hayford, who was to play a role of importance in arousing Gold Coast nationalism, points out in *Gold Coast Native Institutions* (1903) that the Bond made no reference to territorial acquisition. Surprisingly, the Bond, which is always referred to by modern nationalists, is not mentioned by Rev. Carl Christian Reindorf in his detailed *The Gold Coast and Asante* [*circa 1500-1856*] (1889). It is to be noted that when Reindorf, an African, refers to "the Gold Coast nation" and "our country," he means the coastal Fanti. It may be true that both the Ashanti and the Fanti were Akans, but no sense of unity then joined them.

The Fanti Confederation of 1871. These same Fanti chiefs met at Mankesim in 1868 to form a confederacy for mutual protection against the Ashanti. Three years later, after the initial failure, a second conference inaugurated what Padmore terms "the first nationalist movement among the chiefs and people of the Colony." The celebrated Fanti Confederation of 1871 not only called for mutual defense of the coastal tribes, but sought to improve roads, build schools, promote agricultural and industrial projects, tap minerals, extend the jurisdiction of courts, and collect taxes. Though the British mood of these years is reflected in the Parliamentary Committee report of 1865 which had recommended ultimate withdrawal from the West Coast of Africa, they made sure that the Confederation never came to maturity. Shortly after, a re-emerging imperialism saw the British succeed in taking the capital of

Kumasi in the sixth Ashanti War of 1873-1874. For two generations Chief Prempeh's Golden Stool—what the Ashanti priest, Anokye, described as the soul of the nation (*see Reading No. 8*)—was hidden, and it became a factor in an attack upon the British in 1899. Subdued, the Ashantis were officially annexed in 1901 as the Fantis had been in 1874.

The next great expression of modern Gold Coast nationalism after the Confederation of 1871 came as a consequence of the Land Bill of 1897, which would have given the Crown control of the forests. Though not conceived of as a body advocating self-government, The Gold Coast Aborigines' Rights Protection Society (1897) did bring the chiefs and educated classes together successfully to protest the Bill and to promote unity among all the people of the Gold Coast. The deputation of 1898 also requested that they should be permitted to participate in the work of legislating for the Colony.

Casely Hayford. Casely Hayford, lawyer and scholar, writing in 1903, describes the era from 1868 on as "the most pregnant period of our national history." He goes on to say: "With hardly sixty years' educational advantages, we have a remarkable band of able men in all walks of life, a sign of the coming greatness of the people in the new century and in the new civilisation. We only ask for opportunity, that opportunity being fundamentally the prayer that the Aborigines may now be allowed to take part in the work of legislation for their native land." He asks whether one can imagine the Gold Coast and Ashanti "flooded with knowledge and culture" and the several states federated together in one Union. "The world is moving fast, and the Gold Coast and Ashanti with it." Yet Hayford had his feet in two worlds and registered a protest against "any attempt to deal with him [*the African*] as belonging to a people of no past." Writing in 1911, in *Ethiopia Unbound* he calls for the adoption of a distinctive African dress for the cultured African and says at one point: ". . . though European habits will die hard with some of our people, the effort is worth making." High praise is voiced for Edward Blyden, the scholarly Liberian of the nineteenth century, who opposed African cultural assimilation. In the same book, Hayford has his character Kwamankra say: "The crux of the educational question, as it affects the African, is that Western methods *denationalise* [*italics added*] him. He becomes a slave to foreign ways of life and thought. . . ."

Journalists, as in other lands, were most important in spreading the gospel of African dignity and rights. In fact, the first newspaper in the country—and the first in West Africa—was Charles Bannerman's *Accra Herald*, started in 1857. Hayford has high praise for Prince Brew, who edited the *Western Echo* in the latter part of the nineteenth century, and Attoh Ahuma, editor of the *Gold Coast Methodist*, expressed a nationalist's fervor before World War I. The first African-owned and operated enterprise in the Gold Coast was the weekly *Gold Coast Independent* founded in 1909 and published until 1956. Again, as elsewhere, middle-class professionals in the urban centers formed the initial nucleus of modern nationalist agitation.

The West African National Congress. World War I with its Wilsonian call for self-determination of peoples and the Bolshevik call for the demise of imperialism made Africans impatient with the small concessions of the Clifford Constitution of 1916. Hence, in 1920, Casely Hayford convened a meeting of the important West African National Congress, the first interterritorial political movement in British West Africa. Its resolutions, among others, asked that Africans be permitted to participate in the government of their own country, that chiefs be appointed and deposed by their own people (a slap at "indirect rule"), that racial discrimination be abolished in the civil service, that immigration of Syrians and non-Africans be regulated, and that a university be established for West Africa. Hayford in his speech at the Conference sought to buoy its hopes with a reference to the contemporaneous activities of Garvey's Universal Negro Improvement Association in New York. Yet, his projected image was that of respectability: "We must be firm, we must be outspoken . . . but in everything we do, in the name of Heaven, let us be constitutional." Hayford headed a delegation to London in 1920-1921 to present these requests as those of responsible, middle-class, educated men, but to no avail. While the delegation was in London, the chiefs and members of the now more conservative Aborigines' Rights Protection Society cabled that the delegation was not representative of the Gold Coast chiefs and people. As seen by Martin Wight in *The Gold Coast Legislative Council* (1947), "Lord Milner was therefore the more easily enabled to reject the petition. This was the first important instance of a divergence of interest between the chiefs and the intelligentsia."

Provincial Councils of Chiefs. The split between the middle-class nationalists and the chiefs came out also in the controversy over the Provincial Councils of Chiefs in the New Constitution of 1925. Nationalists asserted that the excessive power given to chiefs such as Nana Sir Ofari Atta was intended by the British to divide African society. Bitterly, *The Gold Coast Leader* said in 1926: "The issue is one of life and death for us, for if you perpetuate the possibility of the return of dummies (chiefs) to the legislature, our national independence [*sic*] is gone forever. Probably that is what has been aimed at all the time."

James Aggrey. For several years after this, nationalist agitation in the Gold Coast and in the rest of British West Africa subsided. One figure, J. E. Kwegyir Aggrey, stands out during the 1920's as appealing to all sections of Gold Coast opinion and as especially attractive to Europeans. The Rev. A. Phelps Stokes, reporting in 1934, says that he could not remember visiting a single native school in the Union of South Africa, the Rhodesias, or the East Coast where a picture of Aggrey was not given a prominent position. Aggrey had been made principal of the new Achimota College after having studied and taught for many years in North Carolina. His famous proverb about the necessity for using both black and white keys in producing harmony on the piano (*see Reading No. 9*) brought sentimental praise from the Governor of the Gold Coast, Sir Gordon Guggisberg, who has written that Aggrey felt that "any changes that came to his people must not alter their personality, their spirit as *Africans.*" Yet in Edwin Smith's *Aggrey of Africa* (1930) his words criticize "Uncle Tomism." "There is a Youth Movement coming in Africa that some day may startle the world. This restlessness all over Africa stands for self-discovery, self-realisation. It tells of power breaking through. The great continent has been asleep for a long time. It is now waking up. . . . The Africa of twenty years ago is now gone and gone forever. There is a new Africa coming today and it is a challenge to civilisation."

The Cocoa "Hold-up." Nationalist activity lessened somewhat after the controversy over the Provincial Councils Act of 1925, but was strong enough in 1934 to have the Governor issue an ordinance against sedition. Flamboyant journalism such as in that of the Nigerian Dr. Nnamdi Azikiwe's *African Morning Post* (1934) kept the pot warm. A last major expression of Gold Coast solidarity before the war occurred when cocoa farmers in the Colony and Ashanti "held up" their products in a boycott of European firms. The unity and discipline of the farmers in 1937-1938 brought the economy to a halt and presaged Nkrumah's later "positive action." Bourret in *Ghana: The Road to Independence, 1919-57* (1960) remarks that a result of the cocoa "hold-up" was a renewed respect shown by the people for their chiefs' leadership. World War II, however, was definitely to shift the source of leadership to urban groups and accelerate the striving for self-government.

That intense striving, it must be emphasized, was presaged by *prewar* thought and action. George Padmore in *The Gold Coast Revolution* (1953) calls Casely Hayford "a sort of John the Baptist preparing the way for younger nationalist leaders like Kwame Nkrumah." Ghanaian nationalism was not created *de novo*. In fact, as long ago as 1928 Buell could write: "Because of this very spirit of independence amongst them, the Gold Coast people under careful and imaginative guidance may eventually set an example to the rest of Africa."

Kwame Nkrumah. To a man whose life has been so closely interwoven with his country's destiny, it seemed perfectly natural for Kwame Nkrumah to have entitled his autobiography *Ghana* (1957). The association is not pompous vanity. For if the British were guided by the policy of making concessions under pressure, it was Nkrumah who steadfastly and skillfully directed what had been an ineffectually led Gold Coast nationalism to its fulfillment as Ghana on March 6,

1957. A boyhood hero, Aggrey, says Nkrumah, inspired
him to study in the United States during the depression.
Despite poverty, he passed what he terms a happy decade, studying, working, and eventually becoming a lec-
turer at Lincoln University. But he turned to London
at the close of the war so as to be closer to effecting his
life's goal—the redemption of the Gold Coast and Africa.
After participating in the Fifth Pan-African Conference
at Manchester in 1945, he helped to organize and became Secretary of the West African National Secretariat
(1946) in London. As hopes in the Labour Party's African policies diminished, Nkrumah formed a vanguard
group called "The Circle" pledged to train for revolutionary work in any part of the African continent. In
1947 his years of preparation ended upon receipt of an
invitation from Dr. J. B. Danquah to become Secretary
of the newly formed United Gold Coast Convention
(UGCC).

The Riots of 1948.   After World War II the Gold
Coast had been granted a new constitution as recommended by Governor-General Sir Alan Burns. While it
is true that it gave the country a greater measure of
self-government and united the "Colony," Ashanti, and
the Northern Territories under a single legislature with
an unofficial African majority, the Governor retained
the essential veto power. In Nkrumah's eyes the Burns
Constitution of 1946 conceded too little and too late.
Not long after, inflamed passions erupted in the riots of
February-March 1948. High prices earlier had led to a
peaceful boycott of European and Syrian shops. On
February 28, the day that the boycott was lifted, a
peaceful march of the Ex-servicemen's Union, which dis-
obeyed an order to halt, brought on a clash in which
two Africans were killed and five wounded. This triggered several days of rioting and looting of shops in
which 29 lost their lives and 230 were severely injured.
From that day on says J. G. Amamoo in *The New
Ghana* (1958), the Gold Coast ceased to be a "model
colony." "Later events were to show how grossly incorrect had been the British impressions about the character of the African. Below the apparent obsequiousness,
the tribal differences and the mutual mistrust, there lay a
fervent national consciousness which, properly aroused

and directed, was capable of great feats." As if sensing this, the British detained Nkrumah, Danquah, and other leaders while appointing a Commission of Enquiry, which in the Watson Report of 1948 recommended greater autonomy. Another group appointed to draft suggestions to carry out this aim was headed by an African judge, Henley Coussey, as the British, wishing to exclude radical elements from the committee, denied Nkrumah's plea that Africans select it.

The Convention People's Party. Meanwhile, the freed Nkrumah, dissatisfied with the Coussey Committee, also grew increasingly annoyed with the moderate elements of the UGCC which had failed to impress the masses. He, therefore, by means of speeches and correspondence, through his *Accra Evening News* and other newspapers, by founding Ghana National College and by setting up the Committee on Youth Organisation, became a popular, national figure. All of this was a prelude to the split with the UGCC which took place the month that the Coussey Committee sat. On June 12, 1949, before an audience of 60,000, the largest ever assembled in Accra, Kwame Nkrumah, consummate spell-binder, announced the formation of the new Convention People's Party (CPP) with a demand for "full self-government now." As described by him, the scene at the Arena that Sunday was most dramatic. "The applause which had been tumultuous eventually died away and a deep silence followed. It was a most touching moment for each one of us there. We had decided to take our future into our own hands and I am sure that in those few minutes everyone became suddenly conscious of the burden we had undertaken. But in the faces before me I could see no regret or doubt, only resolution." How was self-government to be realized? "Positive Action" was Nkrumah's reply. Legitimate agitation, employing newspaper and political education, strikes, boycotts, and non-cooperation based upon the Gandhian principle of non-violence, was to bring the British to reason. At the beginning of 1950, after the issuance of the "unsatisfactory" Coussey report which fell short of recommending self-government, Nkrumah began the *Positive Action* campaign. It proved so successful that it led to his arrest. Danquah and the chiefs had turned against him, but as

Nkrumah again was taken into custody he felt that he had the people's support, and neither he nor they would fail each other.

Constitutional Advance. Stewardship of the CPP was entrusted to Komla Gbedemah, who handled it well, though even from behind bars Nkrumah kept in touch with his allies by smuggling out messages on sheets of toilet paper. During the thirteen months that he spent in prison Nkrumah retained his dignity amidst primitive conditions. At its end he was honored by being chosen Leader of Government Business in the wake of the CPP's sweeping electoral victory of February 8, 1951. Upon his release, he declared that he felt no bitterness toward the British, but was unalterably opposed to imperialism. He writes: "We were not fighting against race or colour but against a system." That system, which Amamoo says was "not as despotic and high-handed as some people allege," had now in 1951 permitted another installment on the promised path to eventual self-government. As recommended by the Coussey Committee the Gold Coast was to have extended powers, but not yet the "full" self-government demanded by the Positive Action campaign. Nkrumah, though, now felt that this could be reached more expeditiously through his new position, which at his clever suggestion was re-named "Prime Minister" the following year. It was the Governor, however, who retained control of the civil service, police, judiciary, defense, and external affairs. Nkrumah was able in 1954 to extract from the British a further modification of the constitution giving to the Gold Coast full *internal* self-government. To the belief that the Africans were not capable of it, he replied that the sole criterion of their capacities was their readiness and willingness to assume its responsibilities.

Centralization versus Federalism. The CPP electoral victory of 1954 further entrenched Nkrumah's position, but the field did not remain exclusively in his hands. Symbolic of his purpose was the refusal to recognize an "official" opposition which did not appeal for support on a *national* basis. In his *I Speak of Freedom* (1961) he recalls a speech to the CPP in which he advised opposition parties to "organize themselves and choose reliable and trustworthy leaders—not saboteurs and political renegades and apostates . . . and produce a national policy that the people can accept. They can then contest the elections and let the people decide." Kofi A. Busia, former Head of the Sociology Department of the University College of the Gold Coast who later went into exile, while warning of the "danger of one-party rule" in these years, also cited the need for "awakening and fostering of loyalties wide and strong enough to maintain unity and the responsibilities of nationhood." Fuel for the burning issue of federalism versus the centralized state was added when in 1954 Nkrumah's Cocoa Duty and Development Funds Bill fixed the price paid to cocoa farmers. The frank intention to use funds thus accruing to the Government in an era of high prices in order to expand the *entire* economy did not sit well with those Ashanti who formed the core of the opposition National Liberation Movement. Violence, including the bombing of Nkrumah's house, no more deterred him than what he thought was British official and newspaper favoritism toward the Ashanti. In Ashanti, the chiefs along with those who had been expelled from the CPP for disregarding party discipline, those who opposed "corruption" in government, and those who objected to Nkrumah's economic policies supported the N.L.M. In view of this opposition the British refused to grant self-government to the Gold Coast until after yet another general election. This test of strength in July 1956 again resulted in a decisive victory for the CPP which received 71 out of 104 contested seats. There was no alternative but to agree to Nkrumah's demand for self-government in *all* respects. Opposition leader Dr. Busia, nevertheless, insisted that inasmuch as the CPP had not won a majority in Ashanti and the Northern Territories, a case for decentralization was proved. Nkrumah, of course, considered this ridiculous. The prospect of small, autonomous regions in the modern world was "too unreal to contemplate." Self-determination was not to be confused with fragmentation. In a tone of some exasperation Nkrumah writes that few if any governments in the world exercised so much tolerance and devoted so much time to considering the whims of Dr. Busia's "uncooperative minority as my Government did during these years."

Independence. At long last Ghana came into being on March 6, 1957. Since then, this first of former African colonies to reach freedom, like most other African states on becoming free, has faced no end of problems. George W. Shepherd, Jr.'s judgment in *The Politics of African Nationalism* (1962) is that "Most of Ghana's political difficulties stem from the people's lack of national consciousness." But in another article, Shepherd, first director of the American Committee on Africa, also observes, "The widespread illusion that Nkrumah is losing his grip has little foundation. Most of the people are responding to his programs with enthusiastic support." It is noteworthy that whatever misgivings outsiders have expressed over Nkrumah's methods or goals and whatever doubts have been expressed over the very existence of national sentiment, a decisive majority supported him in leading Ghana to republican status in 1960 and in electing him to the presidency.

Ghanaian Nationalism. What is the nature of Ghanaian nationalism? It has been characterized by anti-imperialism and anti-"neo-imperialism," but no hatred of whites as such, a unitary state, a single-party state headed by a charismatic leader, "African socialism," Africanization of the civil service, nonalignment in foreign policy, support for the United Nations, Pan-Africanism, a warm attachment to past African achievements, and a desire to absorb the best of the world's technology and culture. These clues to Ghana's national destiny are to be found in the attitudes and policies of President Nkrumah, the Osagyefo (Redeemer), the combined Washington and Jefferson of his country. According to David Apter in *Ghana in Transition* (1963): "What is emerging in Ghana in the name of socialism is a national form of traditionalism. This is the reality which lies behind the term African personality. The nation has replaced the ethnic community. The Presidential-monarch has replaced the chief. The authority of charisma has been ritualized into the special role of the warrior-priest." Adulation is heaped upon him in diverse manner (*see Reading No. 10*), with critics pointing to such tidbits as "Lift high the cross of Nkrumah" instead of "Onward Christian Soldiers." But Nkrumah has given evidence of using the popular outpourings for national political purposes, not personal gain. It should be stressed that he sees Ghanaian nationalism as secondary to the wider objective of a united Africa. "To me the independence of Ghana is meaningless unless it is linked-up with the total liberation of the African Continent." The first Conference of Independent African States held in Accra in 1958 was an expression of this goal, and Nkrumah has continually pressed for African political union.

On the international scene, although having received the Lenin Peace Prize in 1962, Nkrumah's foreign policy has been one of noncommitment toward any bloc. "This policy of non-alignment we have interpreted to imply that the Government would act as it sees best on any issue in the light of the country's obligation to the United Nations Charter, our position in relation to the African continent and the Commonwealth, our adherence to the principles enunciated at the Bandung and the Accra conferences and our determination to safeguard our independence, and sovereignty." He has warned against a revival of neo-colonialism wherein African "puppet" leaders sacrifice the interests of their countrymen to those of Europeans. It would seem, however, that his impatience with some of the leaders of the former French territories for their "lackey" attitudes does not sufficiently take account of the people of those countries who have supported, or at least not overthrown, their leaders. The former could, after all, as in the referendum of 1958, have followed the path of Guinea under Touré and rejected the French connection.

The problem of "neo-colonialism" is critical for all newly independent countries. The basic poverty of African lands preceded the European relationship. To interpret the necessity, if one wants to raise living standards, of making concessions to outside capital, whether public or private, as "neo-colonialism" is to stretch meaning out of the word. *The Party* (CPP) of February 1962, in a brief description of "What is Neo-Colonialism?" says that: "The long years of colonial misrule have left the new states with a backward economy. . . . Under the guise of 'aid' the neo-colonialists are brazenly plundering the underdeveloped countries." So long as there is freedom to reject or accept outside terms, then a country is

as free as any country can be in this world. If it is said
that this may mean a freedom to starve, then such may
be the reality of a nation-state world. To say that a man
is a slave because he must eat is semantic arbitrariness.
There are alternatives, e.g., an African common market
or economic coordination, reciprocal economic concessions for mutual benefit of developer and developed, or
national belt-tightening. What independence does give is
the key right to reject or accept the *terms* under which
capital will or will not enter. But that some capital is
needed seems apparent to all.

One may understand Nkrumah's sensitivity over the
nuances of "dependence," but in substance the difference
between himself and, for example, President Houphouet-
Boigny of the Ivory Coast is one of degree. One must
remember that Nkrumah, too, has invited foreign capital
to invest in Ghana, although mainly in large-scale industry. Perhaps one difference between them, aside from
attitudes toward Pan-Africanism and foreign policy, is
the approach to "African Socialism." Here, Nkrumah,
building upon the old African communal spirit and
structure and British Fabian socialism, has added a
modified Marxist socialism in the hope that this is the
most rapid way to span the economic gap of centuries.
The actual structure of the economy embraces both
public and private investment. The mixed economy also
seeks diversification of industry so as to avoid dependence on cocoa. Wishing to shift more of the burden of
belt-tightening onto the artisans through compulsory
bank savings, Nkrumah brought on a strike of railway
and port workers in 1961. Though strikes were severely
limited (the Government preferring compulsory arbitration) this one proved that the road to the welfare state
would not be easy. It is frustrating to those who are
asked to shoulder a burden to hear that a cabinet minister's wife has purchased a golden bed. Nkrumah, himself, has set an example of austerity and declared war on
corruption. "Let our battle cry be Serve Ghana Now.
. . . Fellow countrymen and women, let us build not
only for ourselves but for future generations, a brighter
Ghana which will be an inspiration and shining example
to all Africa."

Evidently not all Ghanaians wish to follow his lead.

Nkrumah, fearing subversion of his program despite majority support, has moved to the one-party state. Opposition has been castigated as being implicated in plots on Nkrumah's life, opposed to national unity, and unnecessary. Simon Dombo, opposition leader after Dr. Busia fled to Europe, charged in 1959 that individuals had been denied freedom of expression and had been intimidated at election time. The next year Nkrumah declared that Ghana's Government was "only an agent" of his Convention People's Party. (*See Reading No. 11.*) Upon introducing the motion for a one-party state Mr. S. I. Iddrissu said that the Ghanaian traditional system had no provision for opposition, but that an unpopular leader could be removed. On September 11, 1962, granting his wish, the National Assembly gave approval to the single-party state. One may be sympathetic to Nkrumah's humane goals, but ask as does Hodgkin in *African Political Parties* (1961): "May the party cease to express the popular will, and what are the tests for discovering when this is the case?" Critics have charged that Nkrumah has used democracy to weaken democracy. His defenders state that Nkrumah is not a minority leader, and that, furthermore, there have been several attempts on his life.

Symbolically, in 1961, the first musical produced and acted entirely by Ghanaians went on tour abroad. Its title: "Obadzeng"—"You Are No Longer an Infant." Ghana's national infancy has passed, but like everyone else it is now experiencing growing pains. But whether or not it succeeds in establishing Nkrumah's "happy society," the world no longer will judge Africa's future exclusively by Ghana's policies. Still Ghana will be remembered by Africans as having been a leader in the emergence of African nationalism. It seems fitting tribute that in December 1962 the First International Congress of Africanists convened in Accra.

6

NIGERIA: FROM GEOGRAPHIC EXPRESSION TO FEDERALISM

"There has always been in Lagos a small band of disaffected persons, ever ready to stir up trouble in the capital or in the hinterland; but luckily the common sense of the people prevents any real harm from being done," writes Sir Alan Burns, Governor of Nigeria in 1942, in his *History of Nigeria* (1948). At another point he continues: "The loud-mouthed demagogue who preaches self-government and independence would be silent if he thought that there was the slightest chance of these things becoming facts. . . ." Burns avoided any discussion or even mention of nationalist or dissident leaders, their parties or programs. The "demagogues" accepted independence only twelve years later. Discontent presaging nationalism began long before independence in 1960 or even when Burns wrote.

The Making of Nigeria. Mixed motives brought the British to Nigeria during the nineteenth century at a time when no such name existed or was conceived. The name "Nigeria" is credited (1897) to the wife of Nigeria's later Governor, Sir Frederick Lugard. With great candor he wrote in his famous *The Dual Mandate in British Tropical Africa* (1929 edition): "It would be absurd to deny that the initial motive for the penetration of Africa by Western civilisation was (with the exception of the religious missions) the satisfaction of its material necessities, and not pure altruism." A treaty with the King of Lagos on January 1, 1852, forbade the export of slaves from this notorious entrepôt, and in 1861 the port and island were annexed. Having received sanction from the Powers at the epoch-making Berlin Conference of 1884-1885, the British proclaimed a protectorate over the Niger Delta and in subsequent years extended it inland. To administer these areas a private company, the Royal

45

Niger, was chartered in 1886. The year 1900 saw the designation of the Protectorate of Northern Nigeria, although further fighting was necessary before pacification was achieved. Finally, in 1914, the amalgamation of the Northern and Southern Protectorates took place to form the Colony and Protectorate of Nigeria. Thus a syncretic union of some 250 tribes with over 200 languages and dialects was established. K. O. Dike, Professor of History and Principal of University College, Ibadan, has written that Nigerian society before the imposition of British power was, politically, "grievously fragmented." "Modern" Nigerian nationalism, in his view, stemmed from this union. "Within this wider unit men's loyalties increasingly became national rather than parochial in scope."

Early Protest Movements. Why and how then did Nigerian nationalism arise? Prior to 1922 no real political party existed in Nigeria. However, there were varied expressions of protest that became the raw material of nationalism. For example, in 1891, on the question of "forced monogamy" an independent United African Church split with the Anglican Church, saying that the "foreign agencies at work at the present moment, taking into consideration climatic and other influences cannot grasp the situation." Methodist, Baptist, and other churches too were rent by schism. In 1914 an African, calling himself the Second Elijah, who had been successful in getting thousands of Africans to forego gin and abjure witchcraft, and before whom chiefs and commoners knelt, was held on charges of sedition. The political implication of these independent African religious bodies was noted in 1928 by Raymond L. Buell: "Religious independence will probably precede political self-government. For this reason these various native churches, which embody the demand for independence, are of political importance." Specific grievances were the motive force behind other protests before the formation of the Nigerian National Democratic Party (NNDP) in 1922. A land tax in 1895 brought out five thousand protesting marchers. In 1908 popular resentment flared over a water rate in Lagos. Writing in 1912 on *The Lagos Land Question,* Herbert Macaulay, who a decade later was to found the NNDP, challenged the Crown's claims to lands in Lagos. Macaulay, generally called the "father of

Nigerian nationalism," expressed "our unbounded loyalty to the British throne." But the "first instance" of the provocation of local disturbance by educated elements took place in 1918 with the Egba Uprising over taxation. Apparently led by African veterans of the Cameroons campaign, it was suppressed by British troops.

Herbert Macaulay. With the end of World War I, the tempo of criticism picked up, voiced by newspapers such as the *Lagos Weekly Record* edited by John Payne Jackson. As in similar situations the British answered with constitutional grants embodied in the Clifford Constitution of 1923. This was the first time that Africans, four of them, were elected to a legislative council in British Africa. Crystallizing educated Nigerian sentiment at this time, the NNDP was formed, with the aim of "government of, by and for the people" though no explicit request for Nigerian self-government was made. Herbert Macaulay, its founder and director, was a civil engineer by profession and grandson of Nigeria's first African Bishop, Samuel Crowther. He was to stamp his personality upon the NNDP and the Nigerian nationalist movement more deeply than any other single figure until Azikiwe, but it is questionable whether Macaulay at this time fully stood for *modern* political institutions. His *Justitia Fiat: The Moral Obligations of the British Government to the House of Docemo of Lagos* (1921) implores "those who have any pride in our native ruling Houses to do their utmost to avert this imminent disaster [*the British imprisonment of Prince Elecko of Lagos and British control of land in Lagos*]." James S. Coleman in *Nigeria: Background to Nationalism* (1960) notes that despite its claim to be "Nigerian" and "national" the NNDP remained primarily a Lagos-oriented organization receiving much of its backing from the market-women. Its years of dominance of the Nigerian "national" movement, the 1920's and early 1930's, were years of expanding education and of the calm before the storm. Perhaps the relative quiet of this period may be explained by the British policy of "indirect rule" which inhibited the spread of NNDP activities outside of Lagos. "Indirect rule," *

---

* Davidson Nicol has wittily written that the British policy of "indirect rule" may have been due to a combination of some wisdom, some malaria, and a little lethargy.

which was Lugard's policy of granting some administrative authority to the Northern Muslim Emirs and giving chiefs power in places, e.g., Iboland, where they previously had none, obviously made "a virtue of necessity." There plainly were not enough Englishmen to govern these peoples directly. In his wartime *British and Axis Aims in Africa* (1942) K. O. Mbadiwe calls indirect rule simply an imposition of the British will through the "advice" of the Resident. As Burns acknowledges, "The Chiefs have little to complain of. . . . The Government recognizes their position and supports them in it so long as they keep within the limits set by their advisors." A further explanation has been offered for the restricted appeal of the NNDP by Chief Obafemi Awolowo in his autobiography *Awo* (1960). In it he states that the NNDP was in no way Nigerian or national, that the "best of its time" was consumed in fighting for the House of Docemo of Lagos. As years passed, the Lagosian intelligentsia drifted away from Macaulay.

The Nigerian Youth Movement. Demonstrating a capacity to join together for common purposes during the interwar era, many tribal and craft unions were formed which developed habits of modern organization. These were later used in broad nationalist fronts, such as the National Council of Nigeria and the Cameroons. One striking example of their activities was seen in the Aba women's riots of 1929, which were started and led by women in protest against the rumor of taxation. Repression by the police cost 50 lives.

Not until 1934 did nationalist agitation begin anew, and then it grew out of ironic circumstances. The Yaba Higher College, unaffiliated to any British university and giving its own *Nigerian* diplomas, was resented by Nigerian nationalists as inferior in status. The resulting clamor of discontent was channeled into the Lagos Youth Movement, which in 1936 was re-named the Nigerian Youth Movement. In Awolowo's words: "The credit for the genesis of political awakening throughout the country, and of fostering this awareness without the slightest appeal to tribal or ethnic sentiments, belongs alone to the Nigerian Youth Movement. When Dr. Azikiwe returned to Nigeria in 1937 he merely strengthened the leadership of the newly emerging Nigeria."

"Zik." It was Dr. Nnamdi Azikiwe ("Zik"), more than any figure in Nigeria, and within a decade in all of Africa, who captured the popular imagination and sparked the national awakening. Through his *West African Pilot* and its string of provincial subsidiaries, his dramatic journalism aroused not merely the Ibo, but Nigerians in all areas. Nine years of study, working, and teaching in the United States had prepared him for his ambitious goal of revivifying Africa. The "Zikism" that was so to animate West African youth was not new, but Zik dramatized it sufficiently to make it seem fresh. His *Renascent Africa* (1937) rings with burning intensity and preaches five ideas: (1) Spiritual balance: "respect for the view of others"; (2) Social regeneration: "African society must be democratic"; (3) Economic determinism: "No longer must the profit motive guide and control the aims in life of the African"; (4) Mental emancipation: "The African must be rid of the inferiority complex and all the trappings of hat-in-hand Uncle Tom-ism"; and (5) National Risorgimento, the right of self-determination. As a member of the Nigerian Youth Movement, along with Ernest Ikoli, Oba Samuel Akinsanya, and Harold Laski's student, Chief H. O. Davies, Zik inspired large masses of people, but antagonized Awolowo. Their rivalry since 1940 has been compounded of differences in personality, tribal background, and tactics. Yet both leaders were anxious to bring about Nigerian self-government. They both supported the charter of the NYM, which saw its principal aim as the "development of a united nation out of the conglomeration of peoples who inhabit Nigeria" and complete autonomy within the British Empire. Awolowo sought, however, to have Zik expelled from the NYM in 1940 on the ground that Zik's "policy was to corrode the self respect of the Yoruba people as a group; to build up the Ibos as a master race; to magnify his own vaunted contributions to the nationalist struggles; to dwarf and misrepresent the achievements of his contemporaries; and to discount and nullify the humble but sterling quota which older politicians had made to the country's progress." Zik resigned. Somewhat grudgingly Awolowo concedes that he was the "first consummate propagandist that Nigeria produced."

As the NYM, in Zik's words, degenerated into desuetude, with Yoruba comprising most of its members, he began the task of welding numerous tribal unions, trade unions, literary societies, professional groups, farmers societies, the National Union of Students, the NNDP, etc., into an over-all program of common action. On August 26, 1944, nationalist efforts were crowned by the birth of the National Council of Nigeria and the Cameroons (NCNC). It culminated years of nationalist agitation. Herbert Macaulay, who brought the NNDP into affiliation with the NCNC, was honored with its presidency while Zik became General-Secretary. Once again, political freedom was to be its goal. Neither the NYM nor the Nigerian Union of Teachers joined it, and its connections with the Muslim North were only through southerners resident there. Despite these limitations, the NCNC was to dominate the nationalist scene for the next dozen years.

Nigeria: Since World War II. One of every six Africans is a Nigerian. Obviously, the process of having artificially welded a heterogeneous mass of some 250 "tribes" and some 40 million people (55 million according to the latest census) into the largest unity in Africa, however tenuous, was accomplished as a by-product of British territorial convenience. But the unity thus created is no more artificial than man's tools are "unnatural." Nigeria is not the first country to exist as a nation-state prior to a ripened nationalism. Cyprian Ekwensi, Nigerian journalist and novelist, has observed that "what remains uppermost in the minds of Nigerians is that impression of a new and growing unity."

Expanding Nationalism. Nigerian nationalism has been and is being shaped by the usual factors: administrative unity of a territory bounded by a French political environment, a communications revolution, a transformed economy, practice in contesting elections, both British liberalism and opposition to British rule, resentment at racial discrimination, and the example of other new nations. Pre-World War II Nigerian discontent was janus-faced as it turned to a reassertion of traditional authority and also to a modernized nationalism. Hugh and Mabel Smythe in their study of *The New Nigerian Elite* (1960) demonstrate that now "contemporary Nigeria is led increasingly by an expanding group of Western-educated and frequently self-made men." The war, which saw 100,000 Nigerians serve in the armed forces at home and abroad, aroused aspirations for a new status of personal and national liberty. Few Nigerians then pressed for immediate self-government, Zik himself in 1943 asking for it in fifteen years. Yet, few nationalists were to be satisfied with the pace of the several constitutional steps toward independence granted in 1946, 1951, 1954, and 1957. Dominion status came on October 1, 1960, and a Republic was proclaimed three years later. One who was satisfied with the staggered progress was Federal Prime Minister, Sir Alhaji Abubakar Tafawa Balewa, who in his Independence Day speech asserted: "Now that we have acquired our rightful status I feel sure that history will show that the building of our country proceeded at the wisest pace. It has been thorough, and Nigeria stands well-built upon firm foundations. . . . Each step of our constitutional advance has been purposefully and peacefully planned."

The Richards Constitution, 1946. The British were not prepared to grant Nigerians responsibility at the end of the war, according to James S. Coleman in his extended study *Nigeria: Background to Nationalism* (1960). Apparently, Sir Arthur Richards, Governor-General in 1945, was either unaware of or indifferent to the bubbling pot. Wartime nationalist activity such as displayed by the Ojokoro youth rally of 1943 seemed minor to him. But a general strike of June 1945, primarily of railway and utility workers, was to make officialdom conscious of discontent and lead to the Richards Constitution of 1946. This first political advance since the creation of the Legislative Council of 1923 failed to placate the more militant nationalists, who saw a distinguishing feature of the Constitution, regionalism, as a stratagem of divide and rule. Professor K. O. Dike of University College, Ibadan, observes that in the main the Richards Constitution encouraged separation. Houses of Assembly for North, East, and West and a new Legislative Council with an unofficial African majority could not hide the fact that their powers were essentially advisory. Nationalists criticized the Governor's reserve powers and the £100 income or property qualifications for

Lagos and Calabar voters. It must be noted, nevertheless, that the Northern Emirs, fearful of the aggressive southerners, Ibos in the East and Yoruba in the West, approved of the change. The North, encompassing over half the area and population but lagging culturally behind the more modern south, had not then developed any noticeable opposition to chiefly dominance. Indirect rule there had absorbed educated elements into the political fabric.

Sectional Disputes. The thorny question of separation versus closer union has dominated postwar politics. While it is true that Nigeria was not a nation before the British arrived, it is clear as Coleman points out that despite British professions of ultimate unity, "The net effect of British policy was to aggravate these differences." Yet, in the Lugard lectures of 1958 a lawyer, T. O. Elias, did pay tribute to the unifying effects of English law on his country. If one believes that the British might have done more to encourage Nigerian unity, advocates of closer union could not hide the continual friction between Northerner and Southerner, between Ibo and Yoruba, and among the smaller peoples. On the surface, Nnamdi Azikiwe, who eventually was to become the first Governor-General in an independent Nigeria and its first President in 1963, and Chief Obafemi Awolowo both favored the National Youth Charter of 1938 which proclaimed the goal of "a united nation out of the conglomeration of peoples who inhabit Nigeria." Zik stood in the forefront of the movement to speed the tempo of self-government and union. Although willing on a limited scale to permit the exercise of local and cultural autonomy, he believed that the division of Nigeria into three large regions "must inevitably tend toward Balkanization." The idea of union, perhaps to its detriment, came most vocally from the Ibo people, who ironically were in a minority. Many Nigerians could not help thinking of Zik as the head of the essentially Ibo-supported National Council of Nigeria and the Cameroons (NCNC). Indeed, he declared before the Ibo State Assembly in 1949 that "the Ibo nation stands solidly behind" the NCNC.

Rivalry and outright animosity between Ibo and Yoruba were to work against a centralized state. Originally, Yoruba Chief Awolowo might write in his autobiography

Awo (1960) that the launching of the Ibo Federal Union
in 1943 was well received by him. "I welcomed this
phenomenon as a worthy means to a great end. If the
members of each ethnic group feel happy among themselves; if they are free within prescribed limits to order
their own lives and advance their culture as they like;
and if the solidarity and devotion exhibited within their
ranks can be sublimated to the cause of the nation, the
federal unity of Nigeria would have been assured." But
when Awolowo returned from study in England in 1948,
he complained of Ibo dominance and played a leading
role in setting up the Yoruba cultural organization, the
Egbe Omo Oduduwa. Yoruba nationalism with a federal
Nigeria was its goal as was the retention but "democra-
tisation" of the system of chiefs. Evidently, the Yoruba
could cite several works such as Samuel Johnson's *History
of the Yorubas* (1897) to affirm their earlier national
history. The Egbe's political expression was the Action
Group, a party founded in 1951 by Awolowo to contest
the election under the new Macpherson Constitution of
1951. Himself a lawyer and businessman, Awolowo
deemed it imperative to keep "complacent reactionary"
politicians then in the Western House of Assembly out
of the new one. The Action Group sought the end of
British rule and called for "the total abolition of want
in our society."

The Macpherson Constitution, 1951. During the
period from 1948 to 1951, nationalist agitation was only
partially submerged by British concessions such as Afri-
canizing more of the civil service, eliminating discrimination in public places, making changes in local government, transforming the University College of Nigeria at
Ibadan, and the retirement of the unpopular Governor
Richards. Advance begat further demand. The Macpherson Constitution of 1951 introduced elections on the
national level for the first time and provided for semi-
responsible government. The central House of Representatives could reject legislation passed by the Assemblies.
But by January 1952 the first nation-wide elections in
the country's history ended in results reflecting Nigeria's
de facto regionalization. Zik's largely Ibo-supported
NCNC won in the East, Awolowo's Action Group in
the West, and the newly reorganized Northern People's

Congress (NPC) under the direction of the Sardauna of Sokoto kept power in traditional northern hands. A democratic Northern Elements Progressive Union (NEPU), associated with the NCNC, offered the NPC only minor opposition.

The Lyttleton Constitution, 1954. Regional discord, as seen in four days of rioting in Kano resulting in 277 casualties, brought about the London and Lagos conferences of 1953-1954 which Coleman refers to as the most fateful deliberations in modern Nigerian history. The 1951 constitution had highlighted centralization with limited powers, but Nigeria now, although with increased regional responsibility, was to be a *federal,* not a unitary state. Somewhat reluctantly admitting that "Constitution-making is not an art in essay writing," Zik well knew the NPC's view that each of the three regions be made practically independent of each other. He acknowledged that federalism had its advantages and referred to Switzerland, the United States and Australia as successful examples of federalism and democracy. Still, he "refused to subscribe to the thesis that we were not a nation, or that we could not become a nation, because of our ethnic and linguistic differences." In the succeeding Lyttleton Constitution of 1954, the Central Government transferred more power to the regional assemblies with a goal of their full, internal self-government. Zik fulsomely praised this latter objective. Whatever reservations nationalists felt about the 1954 arrangements, their falling short of self-government and their return to regionalism, they now sensed that it was only a question of time before independence arrived.

Independence. In 1957 another step in the march toward greater Nigerian responsibility was taken when the Eastern and Western regions were given self-government within prescribed limits and a "national" government was formed by the first Prime Minister, Tafawa Balewa. The latter, a former schoolteacher, had been wary of domination by the south, but during a visit to the U.S.A. had been much impressed by its successful blending of many peoples into a common citizenship. He wrote to a friend from a Manhattan hotel room in 1955: "I am a changed man from today. Until now I never really believed Nigeria could be one united country. But if Americans could do it, so can we." The North which had asked for and gotten self-rule in its area in 1959 had come to accept independence within a *federal* framework. It came on October 1, 1960. Of course, there were and are separatist forces in the Federation. Professor Dike, in 1960, said that it would be dishonest to pretend that harmony existed among the country's leaders. If the average person were asked to classify himself, he might well do so by tribal affiliation. Admittedly, the feeling of nationalism has not matured. Still, centripetal forces are operative. Nigerians, after all, on the third anniversary of Dominion status, did signify their faith in the future by giving their blessings to the establishment of a Republic.

Reflective of broadening nationalism has been the rush to expand education on all levels. By 1962 four new universities were being formed in addition to the existing one at Ibadan. By 1963 there were over 2.5 million children at some 17,000 schools, and over 25,000 were enrolled at teacher training colleges. Since 1958 several thousand prospective teachers have been indirectly aided by Ohio State University alone. Some of the $225 million pledged by the U.S. to Nigeria for its Six-year Plan will go for education. Nationalism will be fostered in the process. The Six-year Plan itself involves national as well as regional planning. In his budget speech of 1962 the Federal Finance Minister said that he saw a vision of a new and prosperous Nigeria. "For the first time in our history an effort is being made to look at the resources and priorities from an . . . all-Nigeria perspective."

Another force strengthening allegiance to Nigeria has been the pride in being a citizen of Africa's most populous and important country. Generally, an attempt has been made to continue the English political heritage. On the second anniversary of independence Governor-General Azikiwe described Nigeria's faith in liberal democracy; a written constitution; freedom of expression, conscience, association and movement; freedom of political parties to organize; and constitutional means to bring about change. "This is a healthy and desireable method of demonstrating to the world our political maturity." In self-praise he also observed that these freedoms "characterize Nigeria as a model state in Africa and portray

our country as an island of reason and tolerance in the
sea of bigotry and intolerance." By way of underscoring
these ideals, a proposed preventive detention act was
defeated in July 1963. That it might even have been
considered may be explained by disturbances in the
Western Region in 1962 and the subsequent treason trial
of Chief Awolowo.

The Arrest of Awolowo. The NPC in coalition
with the NCNC (now standing for National Council of
Nigerian Citizens) has ruled the country since the 1959
elections. At one time that would have been thought an
unholy alliance, but both parties have made compromises in forming the middle-of-the-road government.
Oddly, Awolowo, in opposition, became associated with
a more radical view in attacking the ruling coalition. In
earlier years it was Zik who had said that one must not
forget the masses. Now Awolowo was to advocate African socialism and Pan-Africanism in a way that recalled
Nkrumah. In 1962, after a dispute within the Action
Group over the premiership of the Western Region, the
Federal Government stepped in to declare a state of
emergency. Not long after, Awolowo, who had founded
the Action Group and who was the leader of the Opposition within the Federal parliament, along with 24 other
leading politicians, was charged with treasonable felony,
conspiracy to overthrow the government, and illegal im-
portation of firearms. At the conclusion of a sensational
four-month trial, Awolowo, who protested his innocence,
was found guilty and in 1963 sentenced to ten years'
imprisonment. In an article on "The Trial of Awolowo"
in *Africa Today* Stanley Diamond says that legally and
formally Awolowo may have been guilty, although the
alleged plot seems fragile and irrational. But in a deeper
sense, the charge was merely one in a series of steps—
including the creation in 1963 of a new fourth region,
the Midwest state—to weaken the Action Group opposition. This, in his view, is being done by the NPC-NCNC
coalition in fear of Awolowo's appeal to the more "progressive" elements all over the country. The NCNC once
had this appeal. Nigeria, concludes Henry L. Bretton in
Power and Stability in Nigeria (1962), has already entered a period of social-revolutionary pressure in which

moderation may postpone conflict but not produce stability. He believes the surface calm to be deceptive.

Foreign Policy. On the international scene Foreign Minister Jaja Wachuku summarized policy in these words: "We are neutral in everything but in nothing that affects the independence of Africa." Upon the receipt in 1961 of an honorary Doctor of Laws degree in New York, Sir Abubakar said: "We want to side with whomever we think is right, whether Afro-Asian, Western or Eastern countries." Partly by predilection, partly because of its economic connections with the West, the Government has leaned to the latter. Again, this has aroused an impatient cry from those who prefer the Nkrumah approach to foreign policy and African unity. (See Chapter 8.)

In sum, Nigeria's problem of federalism has been complicated by different socio-economic interests, problems of graft, diversity of language, and religious and personality clashes. Yet all joined with enthusiasm—and sportsmanship—in cheering on their favorite son, Dick Tiger, to Nigeria's first middleweight prize-fight championship victory at Ibadan in 1963. The words of the first stanza of the National Anthem chart the path of the future:

> Nigeria, we hail thee,
> Our own dear native land,
> Though tribe and tongue may differ,
> In brotherhood we stand,
> Nigerians all, and proud to serve
> Our Sovereign Motherland. . . .

Ironically or hopefully, the anthem selected by a board of Nigerians, was written by an Englishwoman.

7

SOUTH AFRICA: "PRISONERS IN THE LAND OF OUR BIRTH"

The Problem. "First, the innate capacity of the Bantu, both on the theoretical and the practical sides, is, so far as can be seen at present, of just the same order as that of the most civilised races," writes Leonard Barnes in *Caliban in Africa* (1930). There are others who do not agree and, as Sarah G. Millin observes in *The South Africans* (1927): "The truth is that the white man does not really want the native to think." The combustible situation which has thus resulted has been kept from the explosive point by superior European arms. Unlike West Africa where the ratio of Europeans to Africans is less than one to a hundred, Europeans make up one-fourth of the population, and inasmuch as their settlement goes back three hundred years, theirs is not the mentality of transients. For them, Africans have constituted a labor force for farms, mines, and industry, and except for a few European liberals, segregation of varying degrees is a prevailing obsession. *Apartheid* or *basskaap* as an Afrikaner policy has merely intensified what has existed since Europeans first came to South Africa. And just as European attitudes have not altered fundamentally, so too have Africans continually opposed them. Throughout the nineteenth century recurring Zulu and Basuto wars indicate that Africans did not accept European rule with equanimity.

Urbanization. During the twentieth century the tempo of detribalization picked up and with it came changes in the manner of African protest.* From 1895

---

* E. H. Brookes in his *History of Native Policy in South Africa* (1924) cautions that "Primitive Native Policy was not, as is commonly supposed, a despotism. Under their ancient tribal system, the Native people were not without representation and the wishes of the tribe at all times played an important part in guiding the policy of the Chief's government." The Zulu, Tshaka, and the Matabele, Umzilikazi, were notable exceptions.

to 1922 the number of African students more than
tripled, reaching 251,872; by 1921 there were 455,398
who were literate and more than 6,000 African teachers.
In 1921 there were 1.6 million Christians, or one-third of
the African population. In 1904, 13.4 per cent of the
African population was urban, and the proportion rose to
22 per cent in 1936. That same year Africans made up
38 per cent of the town population. Although lured to
European industry by higher wages, Africans have also
indirectly been driven to work for Europeans. The notorious Natives Land Act of 1913 eliminated existing land
"squatting" and, except in Cape Province, prevented
Africans from owning land outside of scheduled areas.
Not only was one of its intents according to Hattersley
in his *South Africa* (1933) "to force Africans to accept
service with the European farmer," but as De Kiewiet
has pointed out in *A History of South Africa, Social and
Economic* (1941): "It is even more clear that South
African rural policies have been instrumental in creating
a great native urban population." But where employers
may have looked to increased cheap labor, European
workers saw only competition at much lower wage
scales.

Religious Protest. Urbanization has been a be-
wildering and frustrating experience for the African, who
has rebelled in several ways. Not being able physically to
drive the European out of the land, and being restricted
politically to the extent that only about 8,000 Africans
(and 10,000 "Coloureds") had the right to vote at the
time of Union in 1909, and only 16,000 when the suffrage was taken from the "Natives" in 1936, Africans
have shown resentment in other areas. One has been in
the realm of religion. Edward Roux in *Time Longer
Than Rope* (*A History of the Black Man's Struggle for
Freedom in South Africa*) (1949) observes that "the
first Bantu mass movement on truly national lines was a
religious one. . . . Though outwardly religious (the
Churches) were also to a large extent political in their
appeal." D. Thwaite, in *The Seething African Pot: A
Study of Black Nationalism, 1882-1935* (1936), reports
that Native Separatist Churches in the Union numbered
272. The first of these appeared in Tembuland in 1882
when an African Wesleyan minister called Tile broke

from the Church and set up an independent but unsuccessful religious association. In 1892 an Ethiopian Church was founded at Pretoria. This same year John L. Dube, a Zulu studying in the United States, who later became the first President of the African National Congress, published a little book, *A Talk Upon My Native Land,* which contained these lines:

> Hail, O Africa, thy ransom!
> Raise to heaven, thy grateful song!
> Last in rank among the nations,
> Thou shalt lead the choral throng,—
> Land of promise!
> Thy Redeemer's praise prolong!

In these years a most effective leader appeared in the person of Bishop Turner. A South African, he visited America, and upon returning was greeted with "delirious" enthusiasm. He ordained 2,000 ministers for the Church of God and Saints of Christ. Turner's cry of Africa for the Africans found expression in: "The black is the race of the future, and one day the black man will wake up and shake off the white man's yoke." Another group, the African Christian Union, founded in Natal by the American Negro, Joseph Booth, included among its aims "To unite Christians of the African race . . . and pray for the day when the African people shall become an African Christian nation." When Turner died and his Church split, one group led by Enoch Mgijima with his Israelite followers became involved in a battle with the police. Enoch had once had a vision which he interpreted to mean that the white man would be destroyed. For several years great crowds of his white-robed followers were permitted to celebrate the peace of Passover at Bullhoek. Friction with the local inhabitants and with the police in 1921 brought on a battle which Enoch had said would be won by the Africans as police bullets were to melt like water. Instead, 200 who offered resistance were killed.

As reported by a governmental commission which investigated these independent African churches: "There is a growth of race consciousness with its natural outcome of social and political aspirations among the Natives of the Union." And in an article on "Problems of

the African Church" in *Thinking With Africa* (1928)
Z. R. Mahabane, President of the Cape branch of the
African National Congress, supported the desire "to worship God in their own fashion and in accordance with
their own religious genius. It is also a direct outcome of
the race consciousness which has gripped the African
peoples." An African Professor of Bantu Studies at Fort
Hare College, D. D. T. Jabavu, whose father's name was
known throughout the African community for founding
the journal *Imvo Zabantsundu* (*Native Opinion*) and
Fort Hare College, also summarizes succinctly: "The old
order changeth; and so we behold today in the drama of
the life of the South African Bantu a slow but sure met-
amorphosis from a primitive conservatism to an aggressive modernism in both political and religious affairs."
Georgina A. Gollock in *Sons of Africa* (1928) notes:
"Not one of the prophets were [*sic*] deserted; they were
removed."

The I.C.U.   *Force* kept the African "in his place"
in South Africa. The realization of governmental power
probably accounts for what Eric Rosenthal in *Bantu
Journalism in South Africa* calls the generally restrained
and responsible tone of Bantu newspapers on political
questions. This was so obvious that except for the Zulu
uprising in Natal in 1906 and the Bondelzwarts rebellion
in South-West Africa in 1922, it was thought more
tactful to resort to the limited political outlets or the
strike. A Nyasaland African, Clements Kadalie, organized South Africa's first big trade union, the Industrial
and Commercial Workers' Union (I.C.U.), in 1920.
Though short-lived, says Leo Marquard in *The Peoples
and Policies of South Africa* (1960), it "gave South
Africa a bad fright." To Kadalie's plea for racial harmony, the European Trade Union Co-ordinating Committee replied with remarkable candor that the European
worker was "haunted by fear of competition with the
great masses of Bantu laborers with their low standard
of comfort. . . . Naturally this abyss yawning at his
feet induces him to demand protection *even sometimes
at the price of gross injustice to those weaker than himself* [*italics added*]. "Workers of the world unite!" cried
the I.C.U. newspaper, and by 1924 it claimed 100,000
members. Kadalie, who professed adherence to constitu-

tional methods, and suspected Communists, was accused of being one. Communists, nevertheless, supported the I.C.U. In 1926 he was arrested. Protests from all over the Union, coupled with rioting, led to his release. Trying to secure the nationalization of mines, industries, and railroads, he attempted also to reassure European workers that "our movement does not aim at a native rising." The I.C.U. split into Communist and moderate factions. By 1927 membership fell off amid charges that a leading union official had profited from union funds. In the crisis which followed an appeal was sent to British trade unions for someone to put the I.C.U. back on its feet. The combined forces of internal rivalry, the inertia of members, and governmental harassment stalled progress in African trade unionism between 1929 and 1942 when General Smuts' wartime government eased restrictions somewhat. Leonard Barnes, in assessing its impact, writes: "the I.C.U., inchoate in design and fumbling in execution though it may be is none the less an integral part of [the] struggle towards the light, a moving, and therefore a memorable canto in the Bantu national epic."

The Bunga. Afrikaner antipathy toward that epic led to restriction and diversion of African dissatisfaction and activity. Skillfully, in 1904, granting permission for a Transkeian Territories General Council or *Bunga,* the government made sure that ultimate veto power remained with the Native Affairs Department. Professor D. D. T. Jabavu complained that the Africans did not have the privilege of selecting men of their own choice, that the Magistrates unduly revised the Council's decisions and that Africans had no control over expenditures. In short, the Bunga was basically an advisory body.

The African National Congress (ANC). Urban Africans were similarly hemmed in. Although technically possessing the franchise since 1852, property and literacy qualifications kept registration down. Brookes, nevertheless, in 1924 points to "evidence of a growing national spirit, a sense of race unity among the South African natives." Urban unrest stemmed, in part, from encompassing restrictions on suffrage, movement, residence, and strikes. To give voice to African discontent

Dr. Pixley Seme took the lead in forming the South African Native National Conference in 1909. It soon gave way to the first important political organization in South Africa, the South African Native National Congress, formed in 1912, which changed its name in 1913 to the African National Congress (ANC). Until banned in 1960 the ANC remained the leading African organization in South Africa. John L. Dube, who renounced his father's chieftanship and studied at Oberlin College in the United States, was its first President; Sol T. Plaatje, who translated Shakespeare's *Julius Caesar* into Tswana, its General Secretary; and P. I. Seme, who received a B.A. from Columbia and a law degree in England, its moving spirit. Its objectives were "to encourage mutual understanding and to bring together into common action as one political people all tribes and clans of various tribes or races and by means of combined effort and united political organization to defend their freedom, rights and privileges; to agitate and advocate by just means for the removal of the 'Colour Bar' in political, educational and industrial fields and for equitable representation of Natives in Parliament." On this last point, *aware that force could not drive out the Europeans, Africans in the Union have been compelled to express their desires within the existing state*. Plaatje's *Native Life in South Africa* (ca. 1916), which is a lengthy, literate description of African discontent, however, was a plea to Great Britain to reassert competency in Union affairs and aid the African against the Afrikaner. "The sublime ingratitude (for the Act of Union of 1909) of the Union Government is well-nigh unbearable!"

But the ANC delegation sent to London to protest the Land Act of 1913 was no more successful than were later petitioners. A strike on the Rand that year resulted in the death or injury of 270 Africans. Further strikes during 1919–1920 of African municipal employees in Johannesburg, mine workers in Natal and the Transvaal, dock workers in the Cape, and elsewhere, according to Buell, showed the African capacity for organization and racial consciousness. Afrikaner opinion only hardened.

If a system of true universal suffrage had prevailed, the Africans' nationalism would have entertained a plural framework including Whites. The latter, however, were adamant about controlling the franchise. Nationalist Party Prime Minister Hertzog, two years after coming to power in 1924, introduced restrictive legislation to take away the Cape Africans' right to vote even though their relatively small number of "qualified" voters frustrated the Africans. Not achieving his goal immediately, Hertzog fought the 1929 election on the basis of the "Black Peril." Ten years after he had introduced the legislation, he secured the necessary parliamentary two-thirds approval for the Representation of Natives Act (1936) abolishing the Cape African franchise. Anticipating its passage, the ANC and other groups in 1935 had created the All-African Convention (1935) to oppose Hertzog's quasi-apartheid goals. Again, faced with superior power the Convention and the ANC which later split with it were reduced to passing resolutions.

However unfulfilled, the feeling of African commonality which Lionel Forman traces back to the homogenizing effects of the Kimberly diamond diggings of the 1870's, was to increase and flow into the post-World War II resistance campaigns. Chief Albert Luthuli, later President of the ANC and Nobel Prize winner, in assessing the ANC during these early years in *Let My People Go* (1962) says: "Little headway was made. Neither then nor now were the white rulers in any mood to listen. Congress put more faith in the reasonableness of its claims than the white man's amenableness to reason has justified. But at least Congress was there. . . . Throughout the country as a whole, resistance was unco-ordinated and haphazard. But it was there, and it arose out of the white's refusal to share the country with us, or to permit us to walk free in our own land."

The Union of South Africa Since World War II. A Zulu poem, "The Pass Office," laments:

> Take off your hat.
> What is your home name?
> Who is your father?
> Who is your chief?
> Where do you pay your tax?
> What river do you drink?
>
> We mourn for our country.

It is a crime in South Africa to advocate political, economic, or social change. The result: by 1963, one of every 236 Africans in an African population over twelve million was in jail. Furthermore, on May 1, 1963, Parliament passed a bill giving the police power to keep suspects in prison for repeated periods of 90 days without specifying the charge. The Dutch Boers, whose own nationalism has a long history, have been intransigent. Through the Nationalist Party they have been in uninterrupted control since Prime Minister Daniel Malan's electoral victory of 1948. Ironically, in a society which Africans find totalitarian and brutal, the government in 1962 permitted free sale of liquor to Africans. Anger, perhaps, may be drowned in it, but African energies since the war have also been channeled into political activity. This has been most characteristically represented by the African National Congress (ANC) and since 1959 by the Pan Africanist Congress (PAC). Both were declared illegal in 1960.

It has not been without protest that three and a half million Europeans, superior in arms and technology, have thwarted the demand for political, economic, and social equality of the twelve million Africans, one and a half million Coloured, and a half million Indians. The character of this protest, as before World War II, has essentially been peaceful, not because of inherent docility, but because other techniques would have been futile. At the time of the 1952 Defiance Campaign the non-European Joint Planning Council admitted that they had to work within "given historical conditions." Edward Feit in *South Africa: The Dynamics of the African National Congress* (1962) bluntly describes the situation: "Faced with European strength, and the frailty of their own movement, Congress leaders realised that violence would be fatal to their cause." Two other factors inhibited the success of African protest. A split between the multi racial nationalism of the ANC and the "Africanist" PAC hindered resistance. So did the Gandhian legacy of nonviolence. Only in small measure does the myth hold that India got its independence by shaming the English conscience. In any event, the Afrikaners have not been reached by moral appeals.

African Restrictions.   African freedom, which before the war was circumscribed, has been limited even more since then. An African in 1963 could not vote, had to carry passes, was restricted to certain areas, might be arbitrarily arrested and detained, was limited in joining unions and in striking, could not attend European schools or universities, was not permitted to marry a European, could be moved to other areas against his will, was denied access to public facilities, could not demonstrate for change, and was confined in many other ways. While theoretically the Afrikaner position of *apartheid* (separate development for Europeans and Africans) sums up the Government's policy, in fact the latter has not taken any major steps to implement that philosophy. What does prevail is domination in a mixed society. Europeans talk of African inferiority and barbarism. Africans talk of European brutality and of the need for equal opportunity. They say that if Europeans fear anything, it is their bad conscience. One is reminded of the tragic duet in Kurt Weill's "Lost in the Stars" based upon Alan Paton's *Cry, the Beloved Country* in which on opposite sides of the stage both groups simultaneously sing of their mutual fear. Chief Albert Luthuli, President of the ANC since 1952, in *Let My People Go* (1962) writes: "We do not desire to shed the blood of the white man; but we should have no illusion about the price which he will exact in African blood before we are admitted to citizenship in our own land."

The "Programme of Action."   How has African nationalism manifested itself during the past generation? In 1943 the Youth League, an outgrowth of the ANC, gave impetus to a more aggressive program. Led by the influential Anton Lembede, it advocated strikes, boycotts, and noncollaboration and helped to push the ANC to a more dynamic position. An anti-Communist, Lembede believed that Africans should rely on themselves, not Europeans, for deliverance. He spoke for the "Africanists" in the ANC. These latter in 1959 were to form the PAC. In 1949, the year after Lembede's death and Malan's electoral victory, the revitalized ANC adopted a "Programme of Action." Its goal was "freedom from White domination, the attainment of political independence," and the rejection of *apartheid*. The ANC which had begun to collaborate with the South African Indian Congress in 1946, was to work with other non-Europeans in the major passive resistance campaign of 1952-1953. Neither ANC nor Indian leadership would let the 1949 Durban riots between Africans and Indians deter co-operation in the struggle against apartheid.

The Defiance Campaign, 1952-1953. The first large-scale effort of the ANC to resist the tyrannical laws took place in 1952. Earlier protests such as pass-burning at Langa location in 1946, a strike in 1949, and demonstrations in 1950 and 1951 were sporadic. Characteristically, the Defiance Campaign was to be nonviolent and a joint effort of the Africans, Indians, and Coloured. As Gandhi would have done, governmental authorities were forewarned and asked to repeal the offensive laws. (*See Reading No. 12.*) These were specified as the Pass Laws, the Group Areas Act, the Separate Registration of Voters Act (removing Coloured voters from the electoral rolls), the Suppression of Communism Act (under which non-Communists also were tried), the Bantu Authorities Act (in which tribal authorities were given advisory powers), and the cattle limitation provisions of the Bantu Areas Proclamation Act. Spokesmen repeated that the struggle was not directed against any race or national group, but against the unjust laws. A manifesto declared that "all people, irrespective of the national groups they may belong to, and irrespective of the color of their skin, who have made South Africa their home, and who believe in the principles of democracy and the equality of man, are South Africans." These clear words have stood as a basic feature of ANC policy. According to the planning, first, selected persons were to defy inequitable laws in the big cities, followed by an increase of the volunteer corps and then by defiance in other urban and rural areas. Partly because of disagreement over aims, economic change was not to be a goal of the Campaign which officially began on June 26, 1952. Volunteers entered locations without permits, went at night without passes, and used "European only" facilities. The main area of support was the Eastern Cape, where 5,719 of the 8,557 resisters were arrested. Leo Kuper's study of the Campaign, *Passive Resistance in South Africa* (1957), states that the Satyagraha form of passive resistance influenced the actual conduct of the operation. It had been difficult enough to coordinate defiance with telephones tapped and mail intercepted. Now Malan's government added stiffer penalties. These, no doubt, were discouraging. As the Defiance Campaign reached its peak, it was marred by riots in Port Elizabeth, East London, and Kimberley. Growing out of relatively small beginnings, they led to the killing of dozens of Africans and several Europeans. Although ANC President Luthuli charged that *agents provocateurs* stirred the violence in Port Elizabeth and Kimberley thus giving the government an excuse for repression, the riots were disowned by the Campaign leaders. In 1953 organized activity was suspended. Ostensibly ineffective, the Defiance Campaign brought the ANC a surge of support. Its paid membership leaped from 7,000 at the start to 100,000 not long afterward.

The Freedom Charter, 1955. Backing for the Defiance Campaign had been received from some prominent Europeans, including Patrick Duncan, son of the former Governor-General. Wishing to capitalize on the enthusiasm generated among Africans and these liberal Europeans, Professor Z. K. Matthews, Principal of the African Fort Hare College, called for a new national convention of "all the people of all races in every town, village, factory, mine and kraal." This was to be a Congress of the People, and again, indicates that ANC nationalism was compatible with living alongside of all groups in South Africa. Professor Matthews had been a member of the Natives' Representative Council set up in 1936 when the African franchise was removed, but had come to see it as a fraud. The Congress of the People, which found obstacles in its organizational path, was able to hold sessions at Kliptown on June 25-26, 1955, until disbanded by the police. Delegates numbering 3,000 attended and ratified a Freedom Charter which reaffirmed equal rights "for all national groups and races." It proclaimed that "All people shall have equal rights to use their own languages, and to develop their own folk culture and customs. All national groups shall be protected by law against insults to their race and national pride. The preaching and practice of national, race or colour discrimination and contempt shall be a punishable crime. All apartheid laws and practices shall be set aside." Although it has been said that activities of this sort and the Bloemfontein meeting in 1956 of African and other clergymen did not represent "pure" African nationalism, but rather non-European unity, one must repeat that African nationalism was not averse to a plural society. On the basis of one man, one vote, they had nothing to fear. Gwendolyn Carter in *The Politics of Inequality: South Africa Since 1948* (1959 edition) says that the Freedom Charter took its stand on the Universal Declaration of Human Rights but its emotive language was characteristically Communist. Its most practical consequence was to arouse the Government to charge 156 African and European leaders with treason in 1956. After a trial lasting several years they were vindicated in 1961.

Other Campaigns. Two other campaigns of the ANC in 1955, although unsuccessful, made the Boer Nationalists ever more zealous in their program of apartheid. In February the ANC opposed the shift of Africans from the run-down African quarter of Sophiatown on the ground that the offer of better houses in Meadowlands was intended to "clear" the land for European use. But as no widespread, determined African resistance greeted the moving, the ANC lost prestige among Africans. Similarly, in the anti-Bantu Education campaign, the ANC lacked the resources to implement its opposition to a separate, less "modern" education for the African. The Act of 1953, it was felt, would keep the African "in his place." If the door to an equal education were closed, Africans would be trained for menial work. In the words of Dr. H. F. Verwoerd, who later became Prime Minister, Africans were to be kept from developing "unhealthy 'white collar ideals.' " A boycott of the schools, however, in April 1955 failed when the ANC was not able to set up enough schools or "Cultural clubs" of its own or run them effectively. Again, the ANC lost face. In early 1957 it recovered somewhat when a one-day strike following a spontaneous bus strike was 57 per cent effective. But a strike in 1958 for a minimum wage of £1 per day failed.

The Pan-Africanist Congress. In the wake of the ANC's lack of success in the Sophiatown and anti-Bantu

Education Act protests, in the dispersal of the Congress of the People, and in the inability to sustain a prolonged effective strike, the "Africanists" within the ANC, followers of the late Lembede, broke with the organization. They assumed that the ANC had been ineffective in appealing to the average African because of cooperation with Europeans, Indians, and Coloured. Thereupon, in April 1959, they formed the more exclusive and aggressive Pan Africanist Congress (PAC) headed by a former teacher, Robert M. Sobukwe. Whites, however sympathetic, were not to be relied on, because they put a brake on African action. A PAC official P. Nkutsoeu Raboroko, in an article in the short-lived periodical, *Africa, South,* explains the Africanist case. "Nationalism demands that the interests of indigenous peoples should dominate over those of aliens, because the country belongs to the indigenous peoples. Socialism demands that the interests of the workers should dominate over those of their employers, because their contribution to the creation of wealth is more significant than that of their bosses. Democracy demands that those of the majority should dominate over those of the minority, because they are a majority." In reply Duma Nokwe, Secretary-General of the ANC, says that the Africanists previously *had* joined with non-Africans in the Defiance Campaign of 1952 whose fundamental feature was "precisely its multi-racial character." He adds that the Freedom Charter's principles of equal rights for all will remain a key objective of the ANC. In any case, the PAC, which is more militant than the ANC, has been no more successful in combating the Government than the latter. In *Guilty Land: The History of Apartheid* (1962) Patrick van Rensburg says that the real reason for the status quo is that it has been so difficult to overthrow. For example, the PAC called for the turning in of passes in March 1960, but the police responded at Sharpeville with the killing of 68 and the wounding of 227 Africans. (*See Reading No. 13.*) It is true that a subsequent "stay-at-home" strike called by ANC President Luthuli was briefly successful in most of the big urban centers, but the Government arrested many leaders and banned both the ANC and the PAC. When in April 1961 at the time of the Union's exit from the Commonwealth as a Republic, another strike was planned, the Government police in a series of raids arrested 8-10,000 Africans and thwarted the effort.

Apartheid. With Republican status in 1961 the Nationalist Party presumably embarked on its more formal program of apartheid which had been bruited for years. But if Africans found themselves confined at every turn, two-thirds of the Africans did come into immediate contact with Europeans every day. They were intricately enmeshed in the economic life of the country. In his pamphlet, *Apartheid: South Africa's Answer to a Major Problem* (ca. 1954) Prime Minister Malan admits that: "Theoretically the object of the policy of Apartheid could be fully achieved by dividing the country into two states, with all the Whites in one, all the Blacks in the other. For the foreseeable future, however, this is simply not practical politics." Alan Paton in *Hope for South Africa* (1958) says that apartheid is impossible: "There is no land for it, there is no money for it, there is no time for it, there is no will for it."

As a gesture in the direction of apartheid it was announced in 1962 that two million Africans in the Transkei territory, which for years had control of minor affairs, were to have "internal self-rule." To give one an idea of the degree of control to be retained by the Central Government until it feels that the Transkei can manage itself, the following responsibilities are to be held back: defence, external affairs, internal security, posts and telegraphs, railways, harbors, immigration, currency, public loans, customs, and excise. The vast majority of Africans are opposed to those "Bantustans." Even if there were no reserved powers, the Africans object to being placed in locations comprising only 13 per cent of the Union's land area. Rebellion is expressed by the underground *Poqo* organization which through sabotage illustrates the increasing level of African anger.

An African journalist, N. Nakasa, asks: "The crucial question for the African now is who will help him out of his predicament?" If Africans are ever to break through the enclosing net, it will be accomplished from outside. Realizing this, determined efforts are being made by the "Addis Ababa" powers to isolate the Union through U.N. action.

— 8 —

THE AFRICAN PERSONALITY,
OR NÉGRITUDE

Négritude and Politics. It has been said that if *négritude* did not exist, it would have to be invented. To its participants, though, it is the distinctive essence of the indigenous African and Afro-American spirit or personality—and not new. On the question of which came first, it may be said that, reinforcing each other, African self-consciousness has yearned for political freedom and the latter has been a stimulus to an ideological and cultural efflorescence. "Culture will therefore be essentially at the service of the fight for national independence," say Cheikh Anta Diop in an essay on "The Cultural Contributions and Prospects of Africa." (*See Reading No. 14.*) Dr. W. E. Abraham, Professor of Philosophy at the University of Ghana, in his *The Mind of Africa* (1962), which is dedicated "to us, the African people," says: "It is a tenet of African nationalism that political independence is a condition of economic, social, cultural, and so spiritual strength." And Aimé Césaire writes in "Culture and Colonisation" that colonialism has been an impediment to the expression of a true African culture which will bloom only when colonialism has ended. (*See Reading No. 15.*) In discussing a projected French-speaking "Negro African Nation" in 1959 Leopold Senghor, the leading African theorist of *négritude,* says he does "not believe that it will ever be necessary to form a *unitary* state" [*italics added*]. He and other advocates of *négritude* nevertheless continually transcend national boundaries in citing examples of African culture and achievement.

The result is an aid to continent-wide African nationalism, or Pan-Africanism. Yet, on whatever level it is to rest politically, its importance, says Ulli Beier, a European teaching in Nigeria, lies in giving "a philosophical basis to nationalism and restor[ing] African self-confidence and dignity." Davidson Nichol, Principal of Fourah Bay College in Sierra Leone, adds, "It is this *négritude* or 'Africanhood' which gives the West African [*and other Africans*] his confidence and his desire for independence instead of assimilation."

Definition. What is *négritude*? To Mercer Cook, an editor of *Presence Africaine,* the leading journal devoted to *négritude,* "The rejection of Western values or the refusal to grant them exclusive and universal priority" is one of its basic tenets. In his absorbing work *Muntu, The New African Culture* (1961), Janheinz Jahn says: " 'Negritude' is nothing more than the conscious beginning of neo-African literature." He sees it as the African Renaissance. "For 'Negritude' was liberation: these authors were freeing themselves from the European paradigm. . . . 'Negritude' was avowal: avowal of Africa. . . . Africa was rediscovered, reawakened; from now on African culture was to, and did, furnish the standards. . . . These writers embraced African traditions." Ndabaningi Sithole, describes the "African Personality" as "a desire on the part of the African people to be and to remain themselves in opposition to being converted into black Englishmen, Frenchmen and Portuguese . . . and . . . the desire to control their own destiny." This contradicts, to a degree, what the same author has to say in his book *African Nationalism* (1959) when he writes: "It is impossible to push this new African back into Time's womb. . . . We are not suggesting here that there is a clean break between the present-day African and his forefathers. We recognize fully a sense of historical continuity, and yet, at the same time, we recognize self-evident economic, political, and social discontinuity between the African and his ancestors. The present-day African has new eyes, as it were."

Perhaps the seeming contradiction may be resolved by Senghor's observation of a generation ago: "We must not be assimilated, we must assimilate; that is, there must be freedom of choice, there must be freedom of assimilation." Hence, if change comes, and all expect it, the basic fabric of African civilization will not be broken indiscriminately. Change is to harmonize with African traditions.

Early Expression. When did *négritude* gain momentum? As far back as the nineteenth century, Edward Blyden had written of the "African Personality." Born in 1832, in the West Indies of Ewe parents, he moved to Liberia and became a well-known Islamic scholar and diplomat. At the founding of the Liberian University, as its first President, he delivered an address, "The Idea of an African Personality," which expressed a good deal of twentieth-century sentiment.

> It is painful in America to see the efforts which are made by the Negroes to secure outward conformity to the appearance of the dominant race . . . we are held in bondage by our indiscriminate and injudicious use of foreign literature. . . . The African must advance by methods of his own. . . . It had been proved that he knows how to take advantage of European culture and that he can be benefited by it. . . . We must show that we are able to go it alone, to carve out our own way. . . . We must not suppose that Anglo-Saxon methods are final, that there is nothing for us to find out for our guidance, and that we have nothing to teach the world.

He ends the address with a clear challenge to the African to improve his condition:

> The suspicions disparaging to us will be dissipated only by the exhibition of the indisputable realities of a lofty manhood as they may be illustrated in successful efforts to build up a nation, to wrest from nature her secrets, to lead the van of progress in this country and to regenerate a continent.

René Maran, a West Indian whose novel *Batouala* won the Goncourt prize in 1921, is usually thought of as having inaugurated the literary movement, his literary and personal influence being widely felt in the West Indies, France, and French Africa. In Maran's introduction to the novel he laments: "Civilization, civilization, pride of the Europeans and charnel-house of innocents, Rabindranath Tagore, the Hindu poet, once, at Tokio, told you what you were! 'You have built your kingdom on corpses. Whatever you wish, whatever you do, you move in lies. . . .' If we knew of what vileness the great colonial life is composed, of what daily vileness, we should talk of it less. . . . It degrades. . . ." The word itself was coined by Aimé Césaire, born in Martinique, but inspirer of the West African literary movement. His *Cahier d'un retour au Pays Natal,* written in 1939, provoked wide interest when republished in 1947 with an introduction by the surrealist poet André Breton. In it are the oft-cited lines singing with irony and affirmation:

> Hurray for those who never invented anything
> Hurray for those who never explored anything
> For those who never conquered anything
> But, who, caught, give themselves to the essence
>   of things
> Ignorant of surfaces, but seized by the rhythm of things
> Indifferent to conquest, but playing the play of the
>   world. . . .

Leopold Senghor. Senghor has elaborated, with sophistication, upon the elements of *négritude* in two important addresses delivered before the pivotal First and Second Congresses of Negro Writers and Artists, held in Paris (1956) and Rome (1959). (*See Reading No. 16.*) He sees the European as viewing life from an analytical, exterior perspective, seeking to utilize, conquer, and even kill objects. The African, however, projects himself into sympathetic symbiosis with nature to understand it. *"Le nègre est tout autre. . . . C'est dans sa subjectivité, au bout de ses organes sensoriels qu'il decouvre l'Autre. . . . Voici donc le Negro-Africain qui sympathise et s'identifie, qui meurt à soi pour renaître dans l'Autre. Il n'assimile pas, il s'assimile. Il vit avec l'Autre en symbiose. . . ."* In Senghor's judgment:

> The African Negro image is not an equation-image, but an analogy-image, a surrealist image. . . . The object does not signify what it represents, but what it suggests, what it creates. . . . An image, however, does not achieve its effect with the African Negro unless it is rhythmic . . . it is the rhythm which perfects the image by uniting sign and sense, flesh and spirit into one whole. . . . Image and rhythm, these are the two fundamental features of African Negro style.
>
> He [*the African*] does not realise that he thinks; he feels

that he feels, he feels his *existence,* he feels himself; and because he feels the other, he is drawn towards the Other, to be re-born in knowledge of [*himself*] and of the world. Thus the act of knowledge is an 'agreement of conciliation' with the world, the simultaneous consciousness and creation of the world in its indivisible unity. It is this urge of vital force which is expressed by the religious and social life of the African Negro, of which art and literature are the most effective instruments. And the poet sings: "Hail to the perfect circle of the world and ultimate concord!"

Anticipating criticism, Senghor writes:

I shall be told that the spirit of the Civilisation and the laws of African Negro Culture, as I have expounded them, are not peculiar to the African Negro, but are common to other peoples as well. I do not deny it. Each people unites in its own aspect the diverse features of mankind's condition. But I assert that these features will nowhere be found united in such equilibrium and such enlightenment, and that rhythm reigns nowhere so despotically.

The spirit of African Negro civilisation consciously or not, animates the best Negro artists and writers of to-day, whether they come from Africa or America. So far as they are conscious of African Negro culture and are inspired by it they are elevated in the international scale; so far as they turn their backs on Africa the mother they degenerate and become feeble. . . . That does not mean that the Negro artists and writers of to-day must turn their backs on reality and refuse to interpret the social realities of their background, their race, their nation, their class, far from it. We have seen that the spirit of African Negro civilisation became incarnate in the most day-to-day realities. But always it transcends these realities so as to express the meaning of the world.

Senghor is not merely an expositor of the African spirit, he is one of its leading poets. "New York" has been called "something like a manifesto of *négritude.*" (*See Reading No. 17.*)

Expressions of *Négritude.* In 1947 an editorial in the journal *Pan-Africa,* with implicit irony, cried "Wanted —African Authors!" By 1961 there were numerous African writers and aspirants, many composing in the style of *négritude,* many writing about it. An opportunity for African writers in English to meet came at the first African Writers' Conference in June 1962 at Makerere University College, Uganda. The Kampala monthly *Tran-*

sition, a new cultural journal, reports that it differed from the earlier congresses of 1956 and 1959 in laying less stress on political discussion. A Kenyan, J. T. Ngugi, refers to those writers as "the black heralds of a new awareness in the emergent Africa." By no means are all writers, much less the average African concerned with esoteric questions of culture and politics. Many, nevertheless, are enveloped by them. Their poetry expresses it. F. E. K. Parkes, a Ghanian, waxes rhapsodic in "Africa Heaven":

> Give me black souls
> Let them be black
> Or chocolate brown
> Or make them the
> Color of dust—
> Dustlike
> Browner than sand.
> But if you can
> Please keep them black,
> Black.
>
> Give them some drums. . . .
> . . . Peal
> Peal loud
> Louder yet;
> Then soft
> Softer still. . . .

and in the last stanza:

> Twerampon please, please
> Admit
> Spectators!
> That they may
> Bask
> In the balmy rays
> Of the
> Evening Sun
> In our lovely
> African heaven!

After getting a degree in medicine from Cambridge University, Davidson Nichol returns to Africa and writes:

> . . . I am tired of grim-faced black-coated men
> Reading the *Financial Times* with impersonal fear,
> Of slim City typists, picking their sandwich lunches

Like forlorn sparrows in chromium milk bars;
Of unfulfilled men shouting the racing editions
As I buy my ticket to Camden Town, N.W.1. . . .
. . . I have gained the little
Longings of my hands my heart, my skin and the soul
That follows in my shadow.
I know now that is what you are, Africa,
Happiness contentment and fulfillment
And a small bird singing on a mango tree. (*See Reading
No. 18.*)

With somewhat less polish, perhaps, but assuredly
with fervor, K. K. Baiden writes in "Africa My Land":

. . . Beyond my Canaan there shall lie my land,
The land that gave me birth, my sweet old land!
The greatest island in the world and one
Whose feats to have been conquered there is none.

. . . And when I'm weary and knocked about the world,
O I'd be back to Africa again,
Where dwelt my soul within its blackish den,
And where my flesh, colder than coldest hell,
Would gain the warmth that rays of Africa,
My land, would give to me, plenty and free.

Patrice Lumumba, assassinated Premier of the Congo,
illustrates the yearning for political independence for the
Congo though his imagery seems drawn from Africa as a
whole:

For a thousand years you, Negro, suffered like a beast,
   Your ashes strewn to the wind that roams the desert. . . .

. . . The whole world, surprised, woke up in panic
   to the violent rhythm of blood, to the violent
   rhythm of jazz,
   the white man turned pallid over this new song
   that carries torch of purple through the dark of night.

The dawn is here, my brother, dawn! Look in our faces,
   a new morning breaks in our old Africa. . . .

. . . A free and gallant Congo will arise from the black soil,
   a free and gallant Congo—the black blossom, the
   black seed! (*See Reading No. 19.*)

Dr. Nnamdi Azikiwe ("Zik"), at present Governor-
General of Nigeria, in a speech in 1946 also availed himself of dramatic rhetoric when he said, "I believe in the

God of Africa. I believe in the black people of Africa.
. . . I believe that there is a destiny for the black people
of Africa, and that such destiny can only be realized
successfully under the aegis of free and independent
African nations. . . . I believe that the God of Africa
has so willed it."

**International Conferences of Negro Writers and
Artists.** Thus far, the focus of expression for *négritude*
has been at the two International Congresses of Negro
Writers and Artists. (Out of these meetings has grown
the Society of African Culture in Paris.) (*See Reading
No. 20.*) Thanks to *Presence Africaine* the Congresses'
proceedings have been published. They comprise dozens
of essays on numerous aspects of the African Personality.
Containing much overlapping, some are rather prosaic,
but some are replete with brilliant *aperçus*. That the
authors use European languages in expressing themselves
does not necessarily mean that they are *déracinés*, out of
touch with the African people. In an article on the problems of intercommunication in Africa Mr. Jones-Quartey
says that intellectuals are making great efforts to com-
municate with the masses. Nor can one say that the use
of European languages makes a mockery of African
nationalism. Nehru, after all, spoke English, but there is
an Indian nationalism. A general feeling of pride runs
through the essays. Though many of them talk less of
what African culture is than the problems it faces in
literature, history, sociology, philosophy, art, music, communications, religion, etc., they give some insight into
African sentiments and tasks ahead. If the tone sounds
shrill at times, it may be in compensation for past suffering and some ignorant European attitudes. What is open
to censure is the belief of some exponents of *négritude*
that Negroes are *biologically* different in their penchant
for rhythm or in their sensibilities. Just as there has been
no proof of superior mentality of any "race," so too,
there is no scientific evidence of any innate superiority
in these respects.

Gerard Sekoto's *"La responsabilité et la solidarité dans
la culture africaine,"* however, contains *"Nous, peuples
d'Afrique, avons de par nos origines une façon differente
de réagir aux impulsions de notre être. Nos moyens de
communication dans la domaine abstraite sont conçus*

plus librement que ceux des Occidentaux." Senghor himself, cosmopolitan in his knowledge and interest in the world, though stating that biological determination is little known, blandly contrasts the Negro with the European, saying that American scientists have shown his reflexes to be more natural, more adaptive. One wonders where Senghor got his information. What also seems odd is his statement that because of their natural abilities, Negroes in the American Army had a higher number in technical services than their proportion of the total population. American Negroes were victims of discrimination in being placed in Quartermaster units. A Madagascan Jesuit, P. R. Ralibera, in his paper on the development of African culture, after describing the African attachment for a harmonious life and the wish to love and be loved, says that Africans cannot live otherwise as long as African blood flows in their veins. By contrast, Taita Towett, a Kenyan, in an interesting essay on the role of the African philosopher, insists that color has nothing to do with mind or heart (*"n'a rien à voir avec le coeur, l'âme ou la volonté"*). And the gist of Bernard Dadié's paper on the fable is to show the similarity to be found in African fables and those of other peoples, making it difficult to speak of separate souls.

As regards history, African men of letters and politics reaffirm that despite the absence of written languages, the oral tradition and other evidence testify to a history in which Africans may take pride. S. Biobaku, a leading Nigerian historian, in commenting on the responsibilities of an African historian says that he must not give a picture that may be distorted through the mirror of an unreflective nationalism. A Marxist historian, M. Achufusi, emphatically says that African historians must do all in their power to educate their peoples in the spirit of true patriotism and to hate all exploitation. Opposed to the belief that Europe and Africa depend upon each other, he believes that unity is a necessity for Africa.

In *Religion en Afrique* Marcus James says that amidst the diversity of culture and geography, there exists evidence of a uniformity in the essence of African religion. He points to the adoration of a Supreme Being amongst the Ashanti and the Kikuyu and the common African belief that there is a spiritual energy which exists in everything. Concerning the Bantu belief of the permeating spiritual energy which animates the world Rev. Placide Tempels in *Bantu Philosophy* (1959) says that the key to Bantu thought is the idea of vital force of which the source is God. "This supreme value is life force, to live strongly, or vital force. . . . Force is the nature of being, force is being, being is force. . . . The origin, the subsistence or annihilation of beings or of forces, is expressly and exclusively attributed to God." A plea for the retention of African myths, seen as mature and symbolic by A. H. Ba, is made in his *"Sur l'animisme."* Not only must Africans retain their culture, but they must build on it so as to contribute to world culture.

Opposition to *Négritude.* There are many Africans and others who deny that there is any cultural unity in Africa. The well-known South African author, Peter Abrahams, in "The Blacks" says:

> What does matter to the tribal African, what is important, is the complex pattern of his position within his own group and his relations with the other members of the group. He is no Pan-African dreaming of a greater African glory when the white man is driven into the sea. The acute race consciousness of the American Negro, or of the Black South African at the receiving end of apartheid is alien to him. The important things in his life are anything but race and color—until they are forced on him. And "Mother Africa" is much too vast to inspire big continental dreams in him.

Abrahams provides an interesting portrait of his friend Jomo Kenyatta after the latter, having spent years abroad, had returned to his native Kenya. (*See Reading No. 21.*) "And then Kenyatta began to speak in a low, bitter voice of his frustrations and of the isolated position in which he found himself. He had no friends. There was no one in the tribe who could give him the intellectual companionship that had become so important to him in his years in Europe. So Kenyatta, the western man, was driven in on himself and was forced to assert himself in tribal terms."

The environmental nature of culture is also brought out by another South African now living in Nigeria, Ezekiel Mphahlele, who writes in *The African Image* (1962) and in a previous article that while there is no

cross play between the literatures of South and West
Africa, and communication between them is nil, he is
the product of European-African cultural cross-impacts.
"To writers and artists in multi-racial communities like
South Africa, of course, *négritude* is just so much intellectual and philosophical talk. What's so extraordinary
about our African traits that there need be a slogan or
battle cry about them? If my writing displays an intensity
of feeling and *therefore* of style (Senghor says *négritude*
has less to do with the theme than style), why should I
imagine that I have a monopoly over such a trait simply
because I am black?" *Black Orpheus,* a journal devoted
to African and Afro-American literature contains a sar-
donic poem "Negritude" by F. A. Imokhuede which
which ridicules his title:

Poor black Muse, since we must, under newlaid laws worship
    at your altar
Before true acclaim and recognition can come our way, I
    have no other
Course than to dance to puppet tunes and 'gainst all con-
    science
Force on your new-tuned ears melody that's strange and
    strained. . . .
Why can't you leave the black Muse alone? Must you make
    rules
And thus standardise and commercialise that which differs
    from prophet to prophet?
I want to be known myself but this is not the means to that
    end
I don't care what people think of my verse, for what I write
    is me—negritudine or not.

In related fashion, Dennis Osadebay, a Nigerian poet
admonishes, "Don't preserve my customs, As some fine
curios, To suit some white historian's tastes." (*See Reading No. 22.*)

Négritude and Others. How may one assess *négritude?* René Piquion in *Négritude* (1961) states that it is
neither an ethereal dream, a banal idea, a vague aspira-
tion, nor a black racism in reverse, but unsympathetic
skeptics may perhaps see it as little more than a laby-
rinthine rationalization of a common "defensive" psychological pattern adopted by people when their cultural
or political existence is threatened. This is touched on

by M. F. Dei Anang, in a talk at the Second Congress of Negro Writers and Artists, who warns against ethnocentrism whether African or European. Many do look beyond *négritude* to a universal setting. Mamadou Dia, Senegal's former Prime Minister, writes in *The African Nations and World Solidarity* (1960) that "without culture, no state is worthy of the name. . . . We shall take care not to remain in the trajectory of closed nationalisms. Self-sufficient culture is no more valid than self-sufficient economy . . . the elaboration of our national cultures . . . will have meaning only in the framework of building a world civilization to be shared by all men." Senghor affirms with earnestness that "Exactly because we must build the civilisation of the universal, we must also find ourselves again, because the civilisation of the universal will be made by the contribution of all. . . . And it is because we do not wish to come empty handed, that we are taking stock of our culture and thus preparing ourselves to assimilate whatever is fertile in other civilisations. . . ." In the same vein run the thoughts of a young Nigerian, 'Bola Ige, who expresses a "new pride in our indigenous cultures" but states that "we certainly do not wish to be immobilized by exhortations to look only on our ancient grandeur." In this sense, spokesmen for *négritude* are repeating what was said by Dr. J. E. K. Aggrey of Achimota College during the 1920's: "Our aim is to take the best in African culture and combine it with the best in the culture of the West."

That *négritude* does have its extravagant claims is something to be expected from emerging nationalism. But other countries too, in their time, have exaggerated their cultural distinctness and importance. At its best, *négritude* seeks ultimate absorption into the *mélange* of universal culture. Ghana's U.N. representative, Alex Quaison-Sackey, in his *Africa Unbound* (1963) writes: "The African Personality . . . without pulling up the roots which nourish it, hopes to create, as a force for world peace and unity, a dynamic political creed." For the postwar period, however, its greatest impact has been felt in providing the intellectual impetus behind African nationalism and Pan-Africanism. In his review of Decraene's *Le Panafricanisme,* Thomas Hodgkin admits that there are obstacles to Pan-Africanism, but says: "What would be more valuable would be to be told what are the pre-suppositions of Pan-Africanists, which give them confidence that these obstacles can be overcome, within a relatively brief span of human history." Their *élan* has been sparked by *négritude*.

— 9 —

PAN-AFRICANISM

Many observers treat Pan-Africanism as a fanciful phenomenon with little likelihood of attainment, charging it with little more than resolution-passing and flamboyant rhetoric. While critics see it as merely the product of the alleged messianic imagination of Kwame Nkrumah, its most persistent and eloquent spokesman, supporters have waxed rhapsodic over its imminence and benefits. The fact that the new constitution of the Republic of Ghana contains provision for surrendering sovereignty to a wider African union may seem to be a personal penchant of President Nkrumah. There is, however, no gainsaying his extensive influence in Africa as a symbolic figure of charismatic proportions. Anyone who reads his interesting autobiography *Ghana* must say that he is a dedicated man.

Obstacles. The focal point of criticism lies in its alleged impracticality and lack of substantial realization at present. Obstacles to its fulfillment are seen by former High Commissioner for the Federation of Rhodesia and Nyasaland, Sir Gilbert Rennie, as: Africa's immense size and physical diversity; the existence of some 40 political entities; the presence of Europeans; differences between the richer and poorer African states; and the divergent ideological pulls of the "cold war." In his view, these factors "make the prospect of a united Africa somewhat remote in present circumstances."

Pan-African Hopes. "In present circumstances," nevertheless, may be inferred by Pan-Africanists as implying its eventual fruition. They point to the scoffing condescension with which African nationalism was treated a scant generation ago, and buoyed by ardent hopes, project success into the future. Not only do they think that a fundamental cultural oneness runs through the Continent, but they abhor the "balkanization" of Africa as an economic and political monstrosity. (*See Reading No. 23.*) On pragmatic grounds and for reasons of sentiment Pan-Africanists see the independence of the emerging African states as a mere way-station on the path to unity. In his *L'Expérience Guinéene et l'Unité Africaine,* Guinea's President Sekou Touré talks of independence of different territories as a precondition of their reunification. Over the years *self-government* for African peoples was one of the key aims of Pan-Africanists and, as such, they may claim a goodly share of triumph in the progress toward independence. Yet, perhaps paradoxically, this very gaining of freedom for *separate* states may well be perpetuated through the force of inertia. In these early critical years of Africa's emergence the twig is being bent, and time may institutionalize much of the status quo. Conversely, however, there is still a good deal of plasticity about boundaries and loyalties.

To Pan-Africanists, there are no insuperable barriers to their dreams of a united, free, and distinctive Africa. Physical handicaps can be overcome by modern technology. Political boundaries are believed to be artificial and transient. Richer states will have to subordinate their interests for the common good. Language differences are to be minimized. "All imperialism" is to be combated and the divisiveness of the "cold war" kept from Africa. As to the Europeans and Asians, they will have to accept the principle of equality of voting or be driven out. There being no exact unanimity of opinion amongst Pan-Africanists, varied views may be found as to tempo, tactics, acceptance of aspects of western civilization, and extent of unity. In any case, they usually agree on the need for bringing about regional unity as a prelude to continent-wide unity. According to the national secretary of the African Union of Students (in

America), Babatunde Williams, the idea as now envisioned is to establish from four to eight supranational states or regional federations. Another young African, once editor-in-chief of *L'Etudiant d'Afrique Noire,* Albert Tevoedjre, while supporting African union, believes regional groups are less immediately "utopian."

Pan-Africanism has been manifest on several levels: culturally, in the expression of and search for *négritude* or the "African personality"; politically, in the various conferences since those in Accra (1958) and in small African unions or ententes culminating in the Organization of African States (1963); economically, in the United Nations Economic Commission for Africa (1958) and in an All-African Trade Union Federation (1961); diplomatically, in the Casablanca and Monrovia "blocs" and at the United Nations; socially, in an All-African women's conference (1960), cooperation of African students abroad, etc. It has been sharpened by common opposition to colonialism in Portuguese Africa, Algeria, South Africa, and east and central Africa. It is further strengthened by moral support from American Negroes (where a reciprocal impact is to be noted). Another fundamental source which may make for unity is facing the common problems of economic survival and advance. Not only does the development of river valleys transcend boundaries, but disease control, labor migration, and transportation may compel some form of cooperation. Whether this will be of an *ad hoc* nature or the harbinger of political union remains to be seen. To illustrate the reverse side of the economic picture, no less a person than Leopold Senghor has succinctly noted that, at least for the present, African economies are more competitive than complementary.

In short, Pan-Africanism while animated by great hopes has achieved moderate success. Its most notable attainment, the formation of the Organization of African States at Addis Ababa in 1963, fell short of more ardent Pan-African dreams. Supporters have accepted this initial step, hoping some day to project it to a new plateau.

Accra Conference, 1958. For a decade after the Fifth Pan African Congress of 1945 held in Manchester, except for continued contact among African leaders and students abroad, very little in the way of concrete Pan-

African activity took place. As noted previously, however, one of the prime goals of earlier Pan-Africanists
was the securing of independence for *individual* African
states. The historic Afro-Asian Conference at Bandung
in 1955 triggered a new momentum in African self-
consciousness. Glad as they were to associate themselves
with non-African countries of similar backgrounds and
problems, many Africans wanted to draw closer together
to assert their "personality" and to control their own
future. Another, smaller Afro-Asian Peoples' Solidarity
Conference took place in December 1955 in Cairo. But
it was not until the First Conference of Independent
African States held at Accra, Ghana, in April 1958 that
Pan-Africanism may be said to have come of age.

If the discussions of *négritude* were more extensive
in former French possessions, where assimilation presumably prevailed, the initiative for political unity came
from Ghana, the former British colony. Ghana having
received Dominion status in 1957, Prime Minister Nkrumah launched his crusade. Invitations were extended to
Ethiopia, Libya, Tunisia, Morocco, Egypt, Liberia, the
Sudan, and South Africa (the latter refusing). In Nkrumah's words: "This first conference of independent
African states was, I think, the most significant event
in the history of Africa for many centuries." Expressions
of friendship and common purpose were voiced during
the week of April 15-22, 1958, with resolutions calling
for unity in foreign affairs, support for Africans seeking
freedom, and the promotion of economic, educational,
and cultural cooperation. Nothing as yet of a common
policy! The speeches rang with the word unity, but not
political union as Nkrumah might have wished. The
Sudanese delegate closed his speech with "Forward
Africa, United, undaunted and determined, till the whole
task is done, freedom won, and all men, in God's bounty,
live in peace." It is true that Nkrumah had set only
limited goals for the first conference such as having
leaders get to know one another personally, the maintenance of newly won independence, and world peace. His
closing address said that: "We should respect the independence, sovereignty and territorial integrity of one
another." This may perhaps have been a tactical move,
considering the fact that he was in favor of more con-

crete union. In any case, biannual conferences were projected for the future, and the symbol for universal African freedom was set in the observance of African Freedom Day on the fifteenth of April.

Addis Ábaba, 1960. Addis Ababa (June 1960) was the site of the Second Conference of Independent African States. Aside from the eight countries previously in attendance, Nigeria, Somalia, Guinea, Cameroon, and Algeria were represented, as were the Federation of Mali, Madagascar, and Sierra Leone. Haile Selassie, head of the host country, welcomed the delegates with a plea for increased African unity as a necessity in furthering African freedom. African countries, he said, must not barter their independence in exchange for foreign support or subsidies. Resolutions passed by the Second Conference included the familiar ones supporting the Algerian rebels, condemning the Union on South-West Africa, condemning France for the use of the Sahara as a nuclear test site, asking for the dissolution of the Central African Federation with freedom for Nyasaland and Northern Rhodesia, and boycotting South Africa for its policy of *apartheid* and discrimination. The Conference also sought economic cooperation among the African states through a proposed Council for African Economic Cooperation, a joint African development bank, and preferential treatment in tariffs with a view toward greater reduction. Resolutions also called for an Air Union, a Council for African Educational, Cultural, Scientific, and Economic Cooperation, and for "unswerving" loyalty to the United Nations. On the basic matter of African unity, a request that the heads of States initiate consultations through diplomatic channels with a "view to promoting African unity" could not hide the fact that the matter was to be inscribed on the agenda of the *next* session of the Conference of Independent African States. In the year of African freedom, 1960, the United States of Africa was still far from realization.

All-African People's Conferences. Along with the two Conferences of Independent States and supplementing their objectives, other All-African People's Conferences have taken place at Accra (December 1958), Conakry

(April 1959) (*see Reading No. 24*), Tunis (January 1960), and Cairo (March 1961). Insofar as not all African states have secured independence, these meetings have given many leaders and potential leaders as distinct from governments the opportunity to enlarge their contacts. Resolutions of the Conference at Accra, after condemnation of colonialism in Africa, recommended, among other things, the creation of an "African Legion" consisting of volunteers who would be ready "to protect the freedom of the African peoples." Another interesting point was the criticism of chieftaincy. "Be it resolved that those African traditional institutions whether political, social or economic, which have clearly shown their reactionary character and their sordid support for colonialism be condemned." At Tunis, George Houser, Director of the American Committee on Africa, reported a more critical attitude toward United States foreign policy. On the question of Egyptian-Ghanian rivalry for leadership, if such existed, he says the Conference implicitly recognized that leadership in the Pan-African movement lies south of the Sahara. Yet Cairo was chosen to be the site of the Third All-African People's Conference.

Held in March 1961, the Conference drew delegates from 54 political and trade union organizations of 31 countries. It assailed the "neo-colonialism" that involved economic dependence of new countries upon their former rulers and capital investments under unequal concessions. It condemned President Kennedy's "Peace Corps" as a threat, designed for economic conquest. The Congo crisis dominated discussions, and the United Nations (which had not forcefully backed the Central Government, as it was to do later) came in for attack. The United States too was criticized, as the tone of the Conference moved, in Houser's words, to an "anti-Western neutralism." Though the meetings may continue for several years to come, the Conference of Independent States will take over its functions. For peoples of European-dominated territories, however, it does provide a most convenient form of liaison with other Africans. Hence, in commenting on the Cairo Conference, *Radar*, published in London by the National Democratic Party of Southern Rhodesia, noted that an interest in the "supreme non-governmental Pan-African Organization [*has*] grown."

Until this point, the two Conferences of Independent States and the People's Conferences had been the strongest expression of formal continent-wide Pan-Africanism. Complementing their work and spirit were other gatherings at Accra in April 1960 called the Positive Action Conference for Peace and Security in Africa and the Second Conference of Afro-Asian Solidarity held at Conakry, Guinea, the following week. Their spirit echoed that of previous assemblages.

East African Federation.   While the initiative for Pan-African unity has come from West Africa, another center for its spread has emerged in East Africa. Here, a *lingua franca,* Swahili, and the common British colonial experience have brought a recent surge toward regional federation. The British-sponsored East Africa High Commission, set up in 1948, and whose responsibilities include transport, postal and telecommunications, customs duties, statistics, agricultural research, and other matters habituated East Africans to think in wider terms. For years African leaders were suspicious of moves toward East African federation, considering them merely a British device to secure tighter control, as in the Central African Federation. But as the likelihood of independence became more real, African leaders formed the Pan African Freedom Movement of East and Central Africa (PAFMECA) in September 1958. It sought to unite Tanganyika, Kenya, Uganda, Zanzibar and Nyasaland, Northern Rhodesia, and Southern Rhodesia. Later, Tanganyikan leader Julius Nyerere at the October 1960 meeting at Mbale, Uganda, showed a willingness to delay Tanganyikan independence if it would facilitate the setting up of an East African federation. That he did not, may have been due to the uncertainty over Kenya's immediate future. For their part, whatever their differences, Kenya's African leaders gave at least qualified approval for federation of East African lands, and the Kenyan Legislative Council in June 1961 agreed that federation of the four lands was economically and politically desirable. Furthermore, President Osman of Somalia, after a visit to Ghana in 1961, expressed pleas-

ure at the concept of a union of East and Central
African states and hoped that such federation would be
the basis for the formation ". . . of an even greater
African union."

At the January 1961 meeting of PAFMECA Mboya,
Nyerere, Kaunda, Nkomo, and other prominent leaders
looked to eventual federation. And at a meeting in June
1963 Kenya's Prime Minister Kenyatta, Tanganyika's
Nyerere, and Uganda's Obote agreed upon federation.
"We have a common history, culture and customs, which
make our unity both logical and natural," affirmed
Kenyatta. The slips 'twixt cup and lip which prevented
unity by the end of 1963 included Ugandan suspicions
of Kenyan domination, border uncertainty with Somalia,
differing economic orientations, and personality clashes.
A step in the welding of mutual bonds has been taken in
the establishment of the University of East Africa in
1961 with newly founded Kivukoni College in Dar es-
Salaam joining with Makerere College, Kampala, and
Royal College, Nairobi. Students—future leaders—will
continue to cross present boundaries. At its fourth meeting held in Africa Hall in Addis Ababa in early 1962
PAFMECA, by broadening its makeup to include Ethiopia and Somalia to full membership as well as the
nationalist parties of South and South-West Africa,
Basutoland, Bechuanaland, and Swaziland, changed its
name to The Pan African Freedom Movement of East,
Central, and South Africa (PAFMECSA). It condemned
the "colonialist policy of divide and rule and maneuvres
to subvert African unity by encouraging the destructive
forces of tribalism, regionalism, reaction and oppor-
tunism."

Voices of Caution. Not all Africans believe conditions to be favorable for African unity, are sympathetic
to it, or wish it to be guided by Nkrumah or Touré.
Liberian President Tubman thinks that "any hasty or
superficial semblance of unity in areas where conflict-
ing issues are not carefully resolved may undermine the
entire structure of any permanent political unity and
retard real cooperative effort." The powerful President of
the Ivory Coast, Houphouet-Boigny, generally thought
of as "pro-French," often has indicated his suspicion of
a framework that might jeopardize the individuality of

the new system and talks of *"le respect de la personalité de chacun."* Doubts about the imminence of political bonds have also been voiced by one of the grand veterans of Africa's struggle for freedom, Dr.Nnamdi Azikiwe, ("Zik") now President of Nigeria. In his opinion ultimate political unity, which he desires, will arrive only if economic and social ties bind Africa's peoples *before* political ones. He is skeptical of the realization of unity in his lifetime. (*See Reading No. 25.*) Tunisian President Bourguiba has cautioned against forgetting that "there is not one Africa, but . . . many Africas." And Senghor adds: "Like President Bourguiba, I believe that a United States of Africa is not something to be achieved overnight. I feel free to say this since I was one of the first to talk about it. . . ."

The Casablanca and Monrovia Blocs. In the year of liberation, 1960, when former French territories, the Congo, Somalia, and Nigeria secured independence, a major rift divided Africa. This rift was symbolized by the *Casablanca* and *Monrovia* (*Brazzaville*) "blocs." Differing attitudes toward policy in the Congo, relations with Europe, the "cold war," and economic orientation brought the march toward union up short. (*See Reading No. 26.*) Above all, however, what split Africa, aside from the question of leadership, was the pace, manner, and extent of unity. A crisis had now been reached in the history of Pan-Africanism. Although these blocs have been dissolved in the new, wider Organization of African Unity (1963), they are worthy of description for historical interest and because their points of view will now be reflected within the OAU.

Former French Africa. Manifestations of what Pan-Africanists would call the "lackey" spirit of the opposition have been expressed at the three major conferences of Brazzaville (December 1960), Monrovia (May (1961), and Lagos (January 1962). While there is no clearcut division in West Africa between English- and French-speaking territories (as witness the Ghana-Guinea-Mali attachment), the Brazzaville powers are motivated by a sense of belonging together in a French-speaking community. Their recent history has been a tangled one; the result for the present is that these new and relatively sparsely populated lands are following the lead of the Ivory Coast in maintaining connections with France. Their rejection of the proffered French grant of immediate independence in the referendum of September 28, 1958, meant only that territories of *Afrique noire* wished to move toward self-government at a less precipitous speed. Independence did come in 1960 for the twelve French African states plus the Trust territories of Comeroun and Togo. During the course of these two years, the West African lands of Dahomey, Niger, Upper Volta, and the Ivory Coast joined to form the *Conseil de l'Entente* (May 1959). In May 1960 a *Union des Republiques d'Afrique Centrale* comprising the Republics of Chad, the Congo, and the Central African Republic was brought into being. Varying connections with France were maintained. The Entente, which may have been "a hasty answer" to the federalist ideas of "Mali," established a customs union, labor, health, communications and financial coordination, and a fund for development, of which the Ivory Coast, the richest, was to provide the largest share. The Equatorial countries and Cameroun also sought to coordinate economic and other affairs.

After their proclamation of independence, these countries of *Afrique noire,* in a series of meetings at Abidjan (October 1960), Brazzaville (December 1960), Dakar (February 1961), and Yaounde (March 1961) moved toward closer cooperation. In the important meeting at Yaounde, a new economic unit, the African-Malagasy Economic Organization (OAMCE), was proclaimed by Senegal, Ivory Coast, Congo Republic, Chad, Gabon, Dahomey, Central African Republic, Upper Volta, Mauritania Niger, Cameroun, and Malagasy. Besides a customs union, there were plans for a common airline and closely linked foreign policies. This attachment toward each other, and in a sense toward France, may have been hastened by their response to the Ghana-led Casablanca "bloc" on such issues as the Congo, Algeria, and Mauritania. The Brazzaville meeting (December 1960), for example, also included President Kasavubu and Moise Tshombe of the strife-torn Congo. Characteristics of the Brazzaville "bloc" were a desire to remain friendly with France, condemnation of various aspects of Soviet policy, compromises on the question of the Congo and Algeria, and opposition to political links with other African states. This opposition to political connections on the part of the Brazzaville countries, paradoxically, has merged their policies for the present. In their search to win support beyond French-speaking Africa, they brought together twenty powers at Monrovia to amplify and strengthen their stand.

The Monrovia and Lagos Bloc. The Monrovia Conference (May 1961) crystallized African suspicion of or antagonism to Nkrumah's policies. Ghana, Mali, Guinea, Morocco, the United Arab Republic (the Casablanca "bloc"), and the Sudan were notable exceptions in a conclave that saw Nigeria, Tunisia, Ethiopia, Libya, Liberia, Somalia, Sierra Leone, and Togo added to the Brazzaville twelve. Three major resolutions emerged from the Monrovia Conference. Foremost, was the assertion that *Africans should respect one another's sovereignty.* Six principles were to govern African relationships: "Absolute equality irrespective of size, population and wealth, non-interference in internal affairs, respect for the sovereignty and inalienable rights of each state, unqualified condemnation of outside subversive actions throughout Africa based upon tolerance, solidarity, good-neighborliness and 'non-acceptance of any leadership' and unity, void of political integration of sovereign African states."

Other resolutions said that material and moral assistance would be given to help free colonial territories, and disputes between African states should be settled by peaceful means. It is also noteworthy that a resolution called for a technical commission to plan economic cooperation and extend it to such fields as education, communication, and transportation. Participants, interestingly, were asked to teach English and French in their schools. As regards Pan-Africanism the Conference's *functional* approach was a slap at Ghana. For his part Nkrumah responded that only a few of the Monrovia states were "genuinely independent." Another meeting of the Monrovia bloc took place in Lagos, Nigeria, in January 1962.

On December 20, a Charter establishing the Inter-African and Malagasy Organization was adopted with ministers to meet yearly and heads of state to confer at least once every three years. Cooperation of the twenty countries would have included stabilization of prices, regional customs unions by stages, coordination of attacks on disease, coordination of educational systems, and a possible boycott of countries that refused Africans independence at the earliest possible date. This became the basis for the OAU in 1963.

The Casablanca Bloc. While it would be an error to classify "blocs" too rigidly, the Casablanca approach may be viewed as having been: more Pan-African, pro-Lumumba (Congolese centralization), more militantly anti-French in Algeria, more socialistic, and in Morocco's case, against an independent Mauritania. If the Casablanca Conference (January 1961) was a response to the Brazzaville meeting two weeks earlier, and prompted by immediate, concrete issues, it subsequently drew its participants together in important ways. As in an earlier meeting at Leopoldville (August 1960), representatives expressed a wish for the territorial unity of the Congo. They threatened to remove their troops at a time when the United Nations seemed to be leaning toward Kasavubu's loose federalism. But beyond that, the assembled countries at Casablanca—Morocco, United Arab Republic, the Mali-Guinea-Ghana group, Libya, and the Algerian rebel FLN—anticipated military and economic collaboration. On July 22, except for Libya and the FLN, they issued a communique that would have established a customs union over five years beginning in 1962. This was later postponed. Plans were made in 1962 for an African development bank with a capitalization of $30,000,000. And on August 29, 1961, at Cairo, they selected an Egyptian commander-in-chief for a joint African supreme command designed to ensure "the common defense of Africa in case of aggression against any part of this continent, and with a view to safeguarding the independence of African States." If their power were to increase in the future, conceivably, it could be used for "wars of liberation."

The Organization of African Unity (OAU), 1963. By early 1963 the Monrovia and Casablanca blocs constituted the two poles of feeling on Pan-Africanism and seemed to be solidifying their structures. With President Touré of Guinea, however, playing the role of behind-the-scenes mediator, the two blocs met at Africa's largest and *most important* conference of heads of state to see whether their differences might be accommodated. From May 22 to 25 speeches rang with common sentiments and problems. President Nkrumah again pleaded for a union of African states with a strong central government. President Nyerere of Tanganyika rejoined that "There is no god who will bring about African unity by merely saying 'let their be unity.'" In the end, facing reality, it was Nkrumah who conceded to the majority. On May 25, 1963, leaders of 30 independent states signed the Charter of the Organization of African Unity (OAU). The Casablanca and Monrovia blocs—though not their attitudes—died.

The OAU establishes an association rather than a federation of African states. This represents an extension of the earlier attitudes of the Monrovia and Lagos meetings, namely, the "functional" approach to unity. The Charter expresses the wish "to promote the unity" of Africa, but affirms the "sovereign equality of all Member states" and "non-interference in the internal affairs of States." Political assassination and subversive activities are specifically condemned. To achieve "a better life for the peoples of Africa" it calls for coordination of policy on political, diplomatic, economic, educational, cultural, health, sanitation, nutritional, scientific, technical, defense, and security matters. The OAU's principal institutions are to be the Assembly of Heads of State, the Council of Ministers (consisting of Foreign Ministers), a General Secretariat, and a Commission of Mediation, Conciliation, and Arbitration. Resolutions are to be determined by a two-thirds majority of the Assembly. A budget is provided for in an assessment according to the U. N. scale. Working languages of the OAU are to be, "if possible," African languages, English, and French.

Thus far, the OAU represents the apex of Pan-Africanism. Being as gracious as he could under the circumstances, Nkrumah, upon his return from the conference, is quoted as saying, "Unity of the African Continent has become a reality. My lifelong dream is here." Actually, an analysis of his dream would reveal a diagnosis of partial wish-fulfillment and still a great deal of frustration. Nkrumah had wanted to seize the tide at the flood in the period of national independence after 1960, but had not succeeded. Yet, it may be that, as John Phillips says in ending his book *Kwame Nkrumah and the Future of Africa*: "Africa and the World have not seen the last of Kwame Nkrumah's influence." By coincidence, the "father of Pan Africanism," Dr. William E. B. DuBois, lately a citizen of Ghana, and who had convened the Pan African Congress of 1919, died on August 27, at the age of 95. Few would have thought that 44 years after the first Congress so much would be accomplished.

African Cooperation. In addition to the formation of the OAU in 1963 one may cite other steps toward economic and social cooperation. Aside from bilateral agreements, a miscellany of meetings would also include the first conference on radio, the press, movies, and television at Rabat in 1962, a conference of 32 African countries on radio and television at Lagos the same year, the first African Railway Congress in Lagos in 1962, the first Pan-African Youth Congress at Conakry in 1962, All-Africa women's conferences, and a conference at Lagos in early 1961 on the rule of law. In 1960 the first West African Games saw a joint team of West African champions pitted against a European and American Olympic squad.

Africa and the United Nations. Certainly, the United Nations, in several ways, has been a vehicle for focusing African desires. At the 1960, 1961, 1962, and 1963 "African Assemblies" of the United Nations, African delegations were quick to join in repeated censure of South African and Portuguese policy. African delegations have shown unanimity also in their anxiety to keep the "cold war" from the continent, with Nkrumah urging an African "Monroe Doctrine." Two U.N. agencies, the Conference Commission for Technical Cooperation in Africa (1950) and the Economic Commission for Africa (1958), have acted to bring Africans together. The purposes of the ECA are to render advisory services and compile data so as to expedite economic advance. It has conducted a conference of African statisticians and a community development workshop, published a ten-year survey of the African economy since 1950 and technical studies, examined African urbanization, and studied commodity stabilization. If one may, in a sense, view the ECA as a body enhancing Pan-Africanism, in another sense, it is a microcosm of African politics. Whereas at the third ECA conference held in Addis Ababa in February 1961 some states were attracted by the prospects of joining with the European Common Market, it was condemned by Ghana, the U.A.R., and Guinea as a menace to African economic cooperation. The latter thought that links with Europe might prevent diversification and industrialization of their own economies. It was generally felt at the conference that aid should increasingly be channeled through the United Nations to minimize any possible threat to African sovereignty. Two months later, in April 1961, 24 African states submitted a comprehensive program for the long-term social and economic development of Africa under U.N. auspices. Their draft resolution called for the ECA to play a greater role in coordinating economic and technical assistance to Africa. The massive infusion of economic aid which the Africans, as a group, called for had been hinted at by different spokesmen for the United States. The year before, Adlai Stevenson, in an article in *Harper's,* wrote of the necessity for the Western powers to coordinate their aid policy toward Africa along the lines of a new Marshall Plan. To be worked out with the African states themselves, the plan, in his words, "could incidentally be an indirect method of drawing them closer together." In March 1961 at the United Nations he called on the African states to take the initiative in drawing up a program for economic development. It was the first time that a major-power representative had gone before the African caucus at the United Nations. Illustrating the interconnectedness of economics and education, both the ECA and UNESCO convened a conference in 1961 on education in Africa, which with a conference on Higher Education in Tananarive in 1962, discussed pertinent problems on a continent-wide scale.

African Trade Unions. Aside from economic cooperation at the United Nations and in their several recent customs unions, Africans have combined in a significant way in the formation of the All-African Trade

Union Federation. Division has not been eliminated
from the African labor movement, but the Charter
adopted in May 1961 at Casablanca did say that member
unions may not be affiliated with international trade-
union organizations. This clause was aimed at removing
from the continent the Western-oriented International
Confederation of Free Trade Unions, which had 22
affiliates in Africa. Defeated as they were at Casablanca,
those trade unions which desired to affiliate with labor
units outside of Africa formed, in January 1962, a new
group called the African Trade Union Confederation
with Tom Mboya one of its Vice-Presidents.

Ghana-Guinea-Mali Union. The driving force behind the AATUF and behind so much of Pan-African
activity came from the Ghana-Guinea-Mali entente.
Formed originally by Ghana and Guinea after the latter
had daringly broken with the French Community in
1958, it was enlarged by the formal addition of Mali in
July 1961. The latter constituted what remained of the
short-lived Mali Federation (1960), which split when
Senegal left it. Coordinated policies dealing with defense,
economic planning, diplomacy, and cultural matters
were directed by their heads of state meeting in alternat-
ing capitals. The union was open to all. In fact, Guinea's
constitution—like Ghana's—says, in Article 34, that:
"The Republic may conclude with any African state,
agreements of association or of community, comprising
partial or complete surrender of sovereignty in view of
achieving African unity." In a speech prior to Ghana's
acceptance of a new constitution and republican status
in 1960 Nkrumah declared; "In the new Constitution we
advocated strongly the principle of African unity. So
deep is our faith in African unity that we have declared
our preparedness to surrender the sovereignty of Ghana,
in whole or in part, in the interest of a union of African
States and Territories as soon as ever such a union becomes practicable. The keynote of the Constitution which
we are putting before you is: One Man—One Vote and
the Unity of Africa; namely, the political union of
African countries."

By way of broadening the tripartite union, in June
1961 officials of Ghana and neighboring Upper Volta
discussed the removal of customs barriers and elimina-

tion of restrictions on the movement of persons. Guinea and Liberia have also had discussions on matters of mutual economic concern dealing with transportation. The Ghana-Guinea-Mali entente had an impact far greater than its population. Nigeria's opposition leader, Chief Obafemi Awolowo, criticizing the Monrovia Conference as convened through the support of certain Western powers, said that Nigeria should join the Ghana-Guinea-Mali union. In the wake of the OAU's formation in 1963, however, the union was dissolved.

Other Unions.   Other proposed unions of African states have yielded modest results. The federation of Ethiopia and Eritrea (1952), the union of former Italian and British Somaliland (1960), the forced Central African Federation (1953-63), the loose Ghana-Guinea-Mali union, the *Conseil de l'Entente,* the Union of the Republics of Central Africa, and the Union of Tanganyika and Zanzibar are all relatively small. In fact, border disputes have not been absent from the African scene. At one time a union of Morocco, Algeria, and Tunisia might have resulted in the long-talked-of North African Maghreb. This now seems less likely in the aftermath of the border dispute between Morocco and Algeria over Saharan iron ore. Somalia, too, has its claims on parts of Ethiopia and Kenya; Morocco is not happy with the new state of Mauritania; Ghana and Togoland once eyed each other suspiciously, etc. Friction of this character, nonetheless, represents more a carry-over of earlier problems than *modern* aggrandizement.

Pan-Africanism's Prospects.   Pan-Africanism has reached a crossroad. What are its prospects? Toward the close of the nineteenth century, H. H. Johnston wrote: "But I strongly doubt whether there will be any universal mutiny of the black man against the white. The Negro has no idea of racial affinity . . . it is difficult to conceive that the black man will eventually form one united negro people demanding autonomy . . ." (*The Colonization of Africa,* 1899). Obviously, the numerous variables affecting Pan-Africanism's destiny demand that all predictions be tentative. Most non-African commentators are skeptical of any substantial achievement for some time to come. Vernon McKay, a close student of African affairs, writes that the idea of a United States of Africa faces too many obstacles for realization except in limited forms, but the feelings behind it are a powerful force which policy makers can ignore only at their peril. By way of summary, he lists the difficulties it faces: different languages, different histories and cultures, different colonial heritages, barriers in transportation and communication, different religions, frontiers, competing agricultural economies, differences between African and European communities, rival ambitions of African leaders, and African nationalism itself, as opposed to Pan-Africanism. To these, one may add other sources of division, the reluctance of richer areas to share with poorer ones, and competing political and economic philosophies. Lord Milverton, former Governor-General of Nigeria, says: "It is no use to blind oneself to the fact that a common African patriotism has no basis in history or tradition. Loyalties are in essence and origin tribal, family or clan." An editor of the *Cape Times,* Anthony Delius, comments: "But after cheering has died down, African leaders are generally found to be saying that 'it will take a long time to come about.' "

These pessimistic forecasts notwithstanding, Pan-Africanists have not lost heart. Anthony Sampson, the former editor of *Drum,* a widely circulated African magazine, has written about the practical difficulties of "Panafrica" that he encountered while trying to extend the magazine's circulation to West and East Africa. "The overriding impression we gained was that one part of Africa was not, except in the broadest issues, interested in the other parts." He denies, however, that Panafrica is a complete myth. "A few events have reverberated through the black communities of the continent with a force that seems to have broken all frontiers. . . ." Similarly, Thomas Hodgkin, in his book *Nationalism in Colonial Africa* (1956), is wary of the existence of unity, but does point out that Africans increasingly are thinking in those terms. "What is important is that Africans . . . have begun to search for some form of unifying belief, or set of beliefs, which will do justice to the common elements in African experience." And Colin Legum in his *Pan-Africanism* (1962), while avoiding predictions as to its future success, concludes that economically and politically the continent has everything to gain from Pan-African planning. In its eulogy for George Padmore, the Ghanian *Voice of Africa* ends with:

His motto was

'Africa United,
You have nothing to lose but your chains,
You have a continent to regain,
Onward to a United States of Africa.'

On October 9, 1961, at the United Nations, Sierra Leone's Foreign Minister forecast that all or most of sub-Saharan Africa would eventually be united in one form of government or another. While conceding differences amongst the Africans, he asserted that Africans were basically one people and would be joined in a union or federation. At the present juncture, it would seem that one or more of the following conditions might act as catalysts: a change of leadership in Nigeria, the former French states, or Ethiopia; a "war of liberation" in South Africa involving an "African legion"; a successful merger in East Africa; or complete collapse of the economies of the present regimes which might then lead to re-integration on a wider scale. None of these is on the horizon.

Africa, nevertheless, has its surprises. The Roman historian, Pliny, many centuries ago observed: "Africa always offers something new."

Summary and Conclusions. New territorial units in Africa have provided the infra-structure within which a sense of identity is emerging, much as happened in western Europe during the past few centuries. But critical observers have also said that national sentiment within the new states has not congealed, that 70 to 80 per cent of Africans are still villagers, that one must not equate the eloquence of educated leaders with the attitudes of the African masses, that in many areas the African's primary allegiance is still commanded by the tribe. Without doubt, Africa's problems are herculean, and nationalism is still in the process of creation, but millions of Africans do think of themselves as members of national states. As religious diversity in the West made for tolerance, so too, multiple tribal diversities may well be an *aid* to nationalism. Similarly, the very complexity and immensity of Africa's problems may strengthen nationalism by producing the psychological cement to forestall the atomization of society.

A generation ago Margery Perham could write in *Africans and British Rule* (1941): "It is difficult to imagine Africans advancing except through the stage of nationhood, even though independent nations in the future may have to yield to new forms of international control and cooperation." Nationalism which originally sought fulfillment in political independence now will be directed toward surmounting the simultaneous hurdles of raising living standards and providing for education and social services. These are no small tasks when one is told by George Kimble, the noted geographer, that no country in Africa has the resources to live up to its aspirations. Furthermore, there are the other handicaps of disease, illiteracy, residual tribal friction, border disputes, self-seeking politicians, dependence upon primary commodity prices in uncertain world markets, rising populations, and rising expectations. There ought to be little wonder, then, that many Africans have defended the one-party state as most closely reflective of Africa's past and best geared to its present needs. Tom Mboya, in 1961, denied that one-party rule would be incompatible with democracy and said that danger would come from a struggle for power between parties. Yet Ignazio Silone, longtime Italian anti-Fascist, has warned against the danger of fascism in the new African states.

African nationalists prefer to describe their outlook as "African socialism," a blend of pre-European communalism, Fabianism, and Marxism. Only under government direction and planning, they say, can an underdeveloped country lift itself by its boot straps. Although obviously sensitive to "neo-colonialism," they recognize that outside skills and money are needed for economic uplift. Leopold Senghor in his pamphlet *African Socialism* (1959) cautions: "We shall not scorn private capital; instead, we shall seek it, whether it comes from France or elsewhere, provided it does not alienate [*our*] rights. . . . [*It*] is necessary for the development of every modern State. . . ."

Out of conviction and realism, African nationalists have affirmed their neutralism in the Cold War while accepting aid from both sides. They certainly are not neutral when it comes to opposing European domination in southern Africa. On issues such as these and economic, social, and cultural matters African countries have joined for common purposes in Pan-African groups, the latest being the Organization of African Unity (1963). The latter is a creation of those who believe in the precedence of economic and functional cooperation over political union. Culturally, African intellectuals have debated their role in arousing, mirroring, and directing the "African Personality" in a way that recalls similar ambivalent discussions in nineteenth-century Russia, the United States, China, India, and other nations. As might have been expected, some voices of *négritude* have been eloquent, a few, strident and lacking in knowledge. This will continue until all men, Africans included, appreciate their fundamental oneness. Aimé Césaire, one of the founders of *négritude,* expresses it poetically:

> Do not make of me
>   this man of hatred
> Whom I can only hate
> And shut myself
>   within a single race
> Though you know
>   my tyrannic love,
> You know that it is not hatred
> That makes me digger
>   of this single race;
> That what I want
> Is for universal thirst
> For universal peace,
> Finally to summon freely
> To produce within its privacy
> The succulence of its fruits.

Part II
READINGS

— Reading No. 1 —

"THIS IS THE HOUR," 1945 *

Taking the Allies' public pronouncements about freedom during World War II seriously, African intellectuals seized the tide at the flood as Mbonu Ojike, a Nigerian studying in the United States, expresses it in this article.

ᛌ ᛌ ᛌ

There are numerous anti-African habits of thought which hinder the realization of progress and happiness in Africa. Along with these habits of thought come unauthorized plans and platitudes and prognostications for the settlement of "the African problem."

European imperialists constitute a unique phenomenon, an effigy in the political, educational, economic, and even religious and social development of Africa. Their demagogues, whether ministers, governors, or other office holders, are charged with the responsibility of maintaining the *status quo*. And naturally, they employ their shrewd hush-hush policy of gradualism and of the you-will-never-get-there technique to retard progress in Africa. They speak of democracy but act imperialistically. They say "we fight for freedom," but they give Africa political servitude and ignoble tutelage. They proclaim religious tolerance, but are themselves the worst examples of religious bigotry and proselytism.

Utterly Fallacious

Thus it is traditionally thought that the African has no political acumen; has neither religion nor the capacity to direct the general affairs of his country. But the records of Africa's past prove how utterly fallacious these habits of thinking about the African are. We are not children in government, education, religion, or social affairs. We are children only in one thing, namely mechanization of our methods of production and distribution, and in militarism.

Only Africans can adequately plan how best Africans can industrialize and develop modern Africa. Even in Africa it-

---

* *Africa, Today and Tomorrow* (New York: African Academy of Arts and Research, 1945), pp. 45-46.

self, Liberia does not plan for Ethiopia, unless upon expressed request; Egypt does not intend to map out Uganda's future for her; neither does Nigeria propose to blueprint for the Gold Coast or Dahomey, her tomorrow. Real Africans do not intrude upon other people's business, because true Africans respect one another's inalienable right and capability to be one's own master.

But what do we see? Non-African elements, now calling themselves "Africans," think that they could introduce the European brand of territorial aggrandizement into Africa. No, Mr. Jan Christian Smuts! Black and brown Africans do not want to be grouped around your Union of South Africa government. Why should any African, or even anybody else, want to federate or amalgamate with a government whose civilized reputation in democracy includes:

These Gems—

1) Denial of franchise to Africans, as return of thanks for the African spirit of hospitality which moved the Bantu to receive the first white man to come there;

2) Abrogation of African land tenure and the consequent overcrowding of eight million Africans and Indians into "reserves;"

3) Color-bar in politics, trade, and industry;

4) Placing the interest of the two million "exotic Africans" above that of the eight million rightful owners of the land of diamond and gold; and

5) Taxing Africans out of existence or into starvation and degradation.

Not long ago, Lord Swinton, the former Resident Minister to West Africa, expressed his altruistic and philanthropic conviction in regard to West Africa's economic future. He saw us as eternal producers of raw material, consumers of foreign manufactured products, the cheapest labor battalion, and a people who must be administered by foreign governors, foreign mayors, etc. I should have said "civilized governors" and "civilized mayors," etc!

Even an experienced minister, such as Colonel Oliver Stanley, should know how administratively impossible, it is for any minister or manager to have the charge of territories too far, too big, too culturally different and fundamentally complicated in their religious, economic, and political philosophies. The best man to serve Americans is an American; the best man to serve Russians is a Russian; the best man to serve the British or any other nation is their own citizen, who knows what his fellow citizens want and how they want it. Consequently, the best man to serve Africans is an African, not a German, an Italian, a Portuguese, a Spaniard, a Belgian, or a Frenchman.

There is no country of Africa which never had her leaders, prior to European invasion. There is none today which is devoid of such eminent leaders in vital fields of human experience. Africans do not have to get Ph. D.'s from Oxford and Harvard before they can be peaceably restored to the control of their own governments. I never remember when Joe Stalin and Chiang kai-Shek got M. A.'s in foreign, or even domestic, universities. In Nigeria, there are scores of kings and career diplomats who could very well do for Nigeria what President Roosevelt does for his country, or what other leaders of the separately recognized members of the United Nations do for their respective countries.

"Liquidate Your Control"!

The hour has come when every dependent African nation should go to its European "master" and say, without malice: "Let us stipulate when and how you would *liquidate your control over our sovereign right*." This we Africans must be ready now to do—as groups and as nations. For Nigeria, the West African Student Union, London, and the West African Press Delegation to the British Isles in 1943, have both indicated something like what I have in mind. But these are not enough. There must come a people's resolution from all the countries demanding complete self-government. I am sure our British friends would not deny us the thing which we and they fight today as allies to preserve. All they need is a specific indication of our demand.

I offer a ten to fifteen years of handing-over of African governments to the responsible Africans concerned. This period is needed to effect an amicable and systematic return of power and instruments of administration to the Africans. It is not a probationary period; it is a handing-over time lag which is consistent with basic principles of administration, whether it be public or private. This period should be retroactive from 1942, when the idea first crystallized here and there.

Then, after African nations have been fully re-established as sovereign states, these 43 different political units within the continent would work from inside out, which implies federation and confederation. I would like to see a West African Federation, a North African Federation, a South African Federation, and an East African Federation. Their territorial boundaries, official language, federal capital, constitution, and other political details can be worked out voluntarily by Africans for Africans. Then it may be that by the year 2005 A.D., the world could realize a United States of Europe, a Pan-American Union, an Asiatic Federation, and a Confederation of Africa.

By 2005 A.D., I would not be surprised if Africa would then be to the world what America is to the world of today —the place to go and get the lendlease goods. Our coal and petroleum, tin and iron ore, manganese and mica, gold and diamond, copper and antimony, rubber, kola, cocoa, palms, cotton, dairy, fruits, and the sands of the Sahara—these and other resources too numerous to mention are already transferring the economic pulse of the world to Africa. Our fertile soil, our enormous reservoir of power, and our communication potentialities, when fully handled by African engineers, farmers, and industrialists could set up pyramids in the Sahara.

The world need not fear African industrialism. We do not intend to rule Europe, conquer America, or annex Asia. We want to be as free as they, and march on with them in dignity and friendship toward neighborhood and brotherhood in man. If the Atlantic Charter, the Dumbarton Oaks statements, the Bretton Woods Conference, the Cairo Declaration, the Moscow Conference, and the recent Crimean "Big Three" meeting could be taken at their face value, we are hopeful that we will be freed. But if they are meant to be interpreted to exclude statehood for dominated African nations, then let everyone be forewarned: That Africa is now totally impatient with her status. She wants freedom from foreign rule so that she may be free to think, plan, and execute for herself. She wants to be free to continue making her contribution—through art, science, industry, philosophy —to the advancement of man in Africa and the enrichment of the general culture of this One World.

— Reading No. 2 —

INDEX TO AFRICAN POLITICAL PARTIES, 1961 *

Thomas Hodgkin is the author of one of the pioneer surveys of African nationalism, Nationalism in Colonial Africa *(1957), and the equally useful* African Political Parties *(1961), in which he lists these 245 parties.*

✓ ✓ ✓

ABAKO, Alliance des Bakongo, *Congo Republic (ex-Belgian)*
Afro-Shirazi Party, *Zanzibar*
AG, Action Group, *Nigeria*
AGV, Amicale Gilbert Veillard, *Guinea*
AIF, Anti-Imperialist Front, *Sudan*
ANC, African National Congress, *Northern Rhodesia*
ANC, African National Congress, *Southern Rhodesia*
ANC, African National Congress, *Tanganyika*
ANC, African National Congress, *Union of South Africa*
ANCYL, African National Congress Youth League, *Union of South Africa*
APC, All People's Congress, *Sierra Leone*
APROSOMA, Association pour la Promotion Sociale de la Masse, *Ruanda-Urundi*
Ashiqqa, *Sudan*

BAG, Bloc Africain de Guinée, *Guinea*
BALUBAKAT, Parti Progressiste Katangais, *Congo Republic (ex-Belgian)*
BCP, Basutoland Congress Party, *Basutoland*
BDC, Bloc Démocratique Camerounais, *Cameroun*
BDG, Bloc Démocratique Gabonais, *Gabon*
BDS, Bloc Démocratique Sénégalais, *Senegal*
BNA, Bloc Nigérien d'Action, *Niger*
BNC, Basutoland National Congress, *Basutoland*
BPFP, Bechuanaland Protectorate Federal Party, *Bechuanaland*
BPP, Bechuanaland People's Party, *Bechuanaland*
BPS, Bloc Populaire Sénégalais, *Senegal*
BYM, Bornu Youth Movement, *Nigeria*

* Thomas Hodgkin, *African Political Parties* (Baltimore: Penguin Books, 1961), pp. 210-217.

Istiqlal, *Morocco*

Jam'iyyar Mutanen Arewa, *see* NPC
Jam'iyyar Naman Sawaba, *see* NEPU
JUVENTO, Mouvement de la Jeunesse Togolaise, *Togo*

KADU, Kenya African Democratic Union, *Kenya*
KANU, Kenya African National Union, *Kenya*
KAU, Kenya African Union, *Kenya*
KIM, Kenya Independence Movement, *Kenya*
KNC, Kamerun National Congress, *Cameroons* (*ex-British*)
KNDP, Kamerun National Democratic Party, *Cameroons* (*ex-British*)
KUNC, Kamerun United National Congress, *Cameroons* (*ex-British*)

Liberal Party, *Sudan*
Liberation Rally, *United Arab Republic*

MAC, Mouvement Autonome de Casamance, *Senegal*
MACNA, Mouvement d'Action Nationale, *Cameroun*
MANU, Moçambique African National Union, *Moçambique*
MAP, Moslem Association Party, *Ghana*
MBPP, Middle Belt People's Party, *Nigeria*
MCP, Malawi Congress Party, *Nyasaland*
MDD, Mouvement Démocratique du Dahomey, *Dahomey*
MEDAC, Mouvement pour l'Évolution Démocratique en Afrique Centrale, *Central African Republic*
MESAN, Mouvement pour l'Évolution Sociale de l'Afrique Noire, *Central African Republic*
MMG, Mouvement [Comité] Mixte Gabonais, *Gabon*
MNA, Mouvement National Algérien, *Algeria*
MNC, Mouvement National Congolais, *Congo Republic* (*ex-Belgian*)
Mouvement Populaire (pre-war), *Morocco*
Mouvement Populaire, *Morocco*
MPB, Mouvement Progressiste du Burundi, *Ruanda-Urundi*
MPEA, Mouvement Populaire d'Évolution Africaine, *Upper Volta*
MPLA, Movimento Popular de Libertação de Angola, *Angola*
MPT, Mouvement Populaire Togolais, *Togo*
MSA, Mouvement Socialiste Africain, *Chad*
MSA, Mouvement Socialiste Africain, *Congo* (*ex-French*)
MSA, Mouvement Socialiste Africain, *French West/Equatorial Africa*
MSN, Mouvement Socialiste Nigérien, *Niger*
MSUS, Mouvement Socialiste d'Union Sénégalaise, *Senegal*
MTLD, Mouvement pour le Triomphe des Libertés Démocratiques, *Algeria*

PDU, Parti Démocratique Unifié, *Upper Volta*

PFA, Parti de la Fédération Africaine, *French West/Equatorial Africa*

PN, Parti National pour la Réalisation du Plan des Réformes, *Morocco*

PNA, Parti National Africain, *Chad*

PND, Parti des Nationalistes du Dahomey, *Dahomey*

PNP, Parti National du Progrès, *Congo Republic (ex-Belgian)*

PNP, People's National Party, *Sierra Leone*

PNV, Parti National Voltaïque, *Upper Volta*

PP, Progressive Party, *Uganda*

PPA, Parti du People Algérien, *Algeria*

PPC, Parti Progressiste Congolais, *Congo (ex-French)*

PPG, Parti Progressiste de Guinée, *Guinea*

PPK, Parti Progressiste Katangais, *see* BALUBAKAT

PPN, Parti Progressiste Nigérien, *Niger*

PPS, Parti Progressiste Soudanais, *Mali*

PPT, Parti Progressiste Tchadien, *Chad*

PRA, Parti du Regroupement Africain, *French West/Equatorial Africa*

PRA-Sénégal, Parti du Regroupement Africain-Sénégal, *Senegal*

PRD, Parti Républicain du Dahomey, *Dahomey*

PRL, Parti Républicain de la Liberté, *Upper Volta*

PRM, Parti du Regroupement Mauritanien, *Mauretania*

PRNM, Parti de la Renaissance Nationale Mauritanienne, *see* Naḥdat al-watanīyya

PSA, Parti Solidaire Africain, *Congo Republic (ex-Belgian)*

PSAS, Parti Sénégalais d'Action Socialiste, *Senegal*

PSEMA, Parti Social d'Éducation des Masses Africaines, *Upper Volta*

PSS, Parti de la Solidarité Sénégalaise, *Senegal*

PTP, Parti Togolais du Progrès, *Togo*

RDA, Rassemblement Démocratique Africain, *French West/Equatorial Africa*

RDD, Rassemblement Démocratique Dahoméen, *Dahomey*

SACPC, South African Coloured People's Congress, *Union of South Africa*

SACPO, South African Coloured People's Organization, *Union of South Africa*

Sawaba, *Niger*

SFIO, Section Française de l'Internationale Ouvrière, *Congo (ex-French)*

SFIO, Section Française de l'Internationale Ouvrière, *Senegal*

SICP, Somali Independent Constitutional Party, *Somalia*

SLPP, Sierra Leone People's Party, *Sierra Leone*

SMNL, Sudan Movement for National Liberation, *Sudan*

— Reading No. 3 —

JOMO KENYATTA ON CONTACT WITH EUROPEANS, 1938 *

Jomo Kenyatta is a living legend in Kenya. Under arrest for reputedly organizing the Mau Mau uprising in 1952, he was paid the extraordinary compliment of having the con-

* Jomo Kenyatta, *Facing Mount Kenya: The Tribal Life of the Gikuyu* (London: Secker and Warburg, 1953), pp. 317-318.

*tending African parties in the election of early 1961 campaign
on behalf of his release and for his assuming the reins of
government. In 1962 he became independent Kenya's first
Prime Minister. In this work, published in 1938, and called
by Professor Malinowski "one of the first really competent
and instructive contributions to African ethnography by a
scholar of pure African parentage," Kenyatta inveighs against
the European encroachment.*

✓   ✓   ✓

But a culture has no meaning apart from the social
organization of life on which it is built. When the European
comes to the Giguyu country and robs the people of their
land, he is taking away not only their livelihood, but the
material symbol that holds family and tribe together. In
doing this he gives one blow which cuts away the foundation
from the whole of Gikuyu life, social, moral, and economic.
When he explains, to his own satisfaction and after the most
superficial glance at the issues involved, that he is doing this
for the sake of the Africans, to "civilise" them, "teach them
the disciplinary value of regular work," and "give them the
benefit of European progressive ideas," he is adding insult to
injury, and need expect to convince no one but himself.

There certainly are some progressive ideas among the
Europeans. They include the ideas of material prosperity, of
medicine, and hygiene, and literacy which enables people to
take part in world culture. But so far the Europeans who
visit Africa have not been conspicuously zealous in imparting
these parts of their inheritance to the Africans, and seem to
think that the only way to do it is by police discipline and
armed force. They speak as if it was somehow beneficial to
an African to work for them instead of for himself, and to
make sure that he will receive this benefit they do their best
to take away his land and leave him with no alternative.
Along with his land they rob him of his government, con-
demn his religious ideas, and ignore his fundamental conceptions of justice and morals, all in the name of civilisation
and progress.

If Africans were left in peace on their own lands, Europeans would have to offer them the benefits of white civilisation in real earnest before they could obtain the African
labour which they want so much. They would have to let
the African choose what parts of European culture could be
beneficially transplanted, and how they could be adapted.
He would probably not choose the gas bomb or the armed
police force, but he might ask for some other things of which
he does not get so much to-day. As it is, by driving him off
his ancestral lands, the Europeans have robbed him of the

material foundations of his culture, and reduced him to a state of serfdom incompatible with human happiness. The African is conditioned, by the cultural and social institutions of centuries, to a freedom of which Europe has little conception, and it is not in his nature to accept serfdom for ever. He realises that he must fight unceasingly for his own complete emancipation; for without this he is doomed to remain the prey of rival imperialisms, which in every successive year will drive their fangs more deeply into his vitality and strength.

— Reading No. 4 —

PATRICE LUMUMBA ON THE INDEPENDENCE OF THE CONGO, 1960 *

Delivered at the ceremonies marking the independence of the Congo, this speech is remarkable for its candor and statesmanship. Though obviously bitter, it is not vindictive. It may dispel the belief held in some quarters that Patrice Lumumba was a man of blood. Lumumba himself was slain in early 1961.

ꜰ   ꜰ   ꜰ

Your Majesty,

Excellencies, Ladies and Gentlemen,

Congolese men and women,

fighters for independence who today are victorious,

I salute you in the name of the Congolese government.

I ask of you all, my friends who have ceaselessly struggled at our side, that this thirtieth of June, 1960, may be preserved as an illustrious date etched indelibly in your hearts, a date whose meaning you will teach proudly to your children, so

* *Africa Speaks,* edited by James Duffy and Robert Manners (Princeton: D. Van Nostrand, Inc., 1961), pp. 90-93.

that they in turn may pass on to their children and to their grandchildren the glorious story of our struggle for liberty.

For if independence of the Congo is today proclaimed in agreement with Belgium, a friendly nation with whom we are on equal footing, yet no Congolese worthy of the name can ever forget that it has been by struggle that this independence has been gained, a continuous and prolonged struggle, an ardent and idealistic struggle, a struggle in which we have spared neither our strength nor our privations, neither our suffering nor our blood.

Of this struggle, one of tears, fire, and blood, we are proud to the very depths of our being, for it was a noble and just struggle, absolutely necessary in order to bring to an end the humiliating slavery which had been imposed upon us by force.

This was our fate during eighty years of colonial rule; our wounds are still too fresh and painful for us to be able to erase them from our memories.

We have known the back-breaking work exacted from us in exchange for salaries which permitted us neither to eat enough to satisfy our hunger, nor to dress and lodge ourselves decently, nor to raise our children as the beloved creatures that they are.

We have known the mockery, the insults, the blows submitted to morning, noon and night because we were "nègres." Who will forget that to a Negro one used the familiar term of address, not, certainly, as to a friend, but because the more dignified forms were reserved for Whites alone?

We have known that our lands were despoiled in the name of supposedly legal texts which in reality recognized only the right of the stronger.

We have known the law was never the same, whether dealing with a White or a Negro; that it was accommodating for the one, cruel and inhuman to the other.

We have known the atrocious suffering of those who were imprisoned for political opinion or religious beliefs: exiles in their own country, their fate was truly worse than death itself.

We have known that in the cities there were magnificent houses for the Whites and crumbling hovels for the Negroes, that a Negro was not admitted to movie theaters or restaurants, that he was not allowed to enter so-called "European" stores, that when the Negro traveled, it was on the lowest level of a boat, at the feet of the White man in his de luxe cabin.

And, finally, who will forget the hangings or the firing squads where so many of our brothers perished, or the cells into which were brutally thrown those who escaped the soldiers' bullets—the soldiers whom the colonialists made the instruments of their domination?

From all this, my brothers, have we deeply suffered.

But all this, however, we who by the vote of your elected representatives are directed to guide our beloved country, we who have suffered in our bodies and in our hearts from colonialist oppression, we it is who tell you—all this is henceforth ended.

The Republic of the Congo has been proclaimed, and our beloved country is now in the hands of its own children.

Together, my brothers, we are going to start a new struggle, a sublime struggle, which will lead our country to peace, prosperity and greatness.

Together we are going to establish social justice and ensure for each man just remuneration for his work.

We are going to show the world what the black man can do when he works in freedom, and we are going to make the Congo the hub of all Africa.

We are going to be vigilant that the lands of our nation truly profit our nation's children.

We are going to re-examine all former laws, and make new ones which will be just and noble.

We are going to put an end to suppression of free thought and make it possible for all citizens fully to enjoy the fundamental liberties set down in the declaration of the Rights of Man.

We are going to succeed in suppressing all discrimination—no matter what it may be—and give to each individual the just place to which his human dignity, his work and his devotion to his country entitle him.

We shall cause to reign not the peace of guns and bayonets, but the peace of hearts and good will.

And for all this, dear compatriots, rest assured that we shall be able to count upon not only our own enormous forces and immense riches, but also upon the assistance of numerous foreign countries whose collaboration we shall accept only as long as it is honest and does not seek to impose upon us any political system, whatever it may be.

In this domain, even Belgium, who finally understanding the sense and direction of history has no longer attempted to oppose our independence, is ready to accord us its aid and friendship, and a treaty to this effect has just been signed between us as two equal and independent countries. This cooperation, I am sure, will prove profitable for both countries. For our part, even while remaining vigilant, we shall know how to respect commitments freely consented to.

Thus, in domestic as well as in foreign affairs, the new Congo which my government is going to create will be a rich country, a free and prosperous one. But in order that we may arrive at this goal without delay, I ask you all, legislators and Congolese citizens, to help me with all your power.

I ask you all to forget tribal quarrels which drain our energies, and risk making us an object of scorn among other nations.

I ask the parliamentary minority to help my government by constructive opposition, and to remain strictly within legal and democratic bounds.

I ask you all not to demand from one day to the next unconsidered raises in salary before I have had the time to set in motion an over-all plan through which I hope to assure the prosperity of the nation.

I ask you all not to shrink from any sacrifice in order to assure the success of our magnificent enterprises.

I ask you all, finally, to respect unconditionally the life and the property of your fellow citizens and of the foreigners established in our country. If the behavior of these foreigners leaves something to be desired, our justice will be prompt in expelling them from the territory of the Republic; if, on the other hand, their conduct is satisfactory, they must be left in peace, for they also are working for the prosperity of our country.

And so, my brothers in race, my brothers in conflict, my compatriots, this is what I wanted to tell you in the name of the government, on this magnificent day of our complete and sovereign Independence.

Our government—strong, national, popular—will be the salvation of this country.

Homage to the Champions of National Liberty!

Long Live Independent and Sovereign Congo!

THE NEGRO DIGS UP HIS PAST*

During the Negro cultural renaissance of the interwar period, an interest in the Negro past emerged, seeking to counteract the conscious or unintentional depreciation of Negro attainments. If at times it led to exaggerated claims of achievement, it did tend to break down the ethnocentrism of some Western historians. The very fine Shomburg Library in New York is named after this pleader for balance.

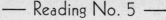

. . . We seem lately to have come at last to realize what the truly scientific attitude requires, and to see that the race issue has been a plague on both our historical houses, and that history cannot be properly written with either bias or counterbias. The blatant Caucasian racialist with his theories and assumptions of race superiority and dominance has in turn bred his Ethiopian counterpart—the rash and rabid amateur who has glibly tried to prove half of the world's geniuses to have been Negroes and to trace the pedigree of nineteenth-century Americans from the Queen of Sheba. But fortunately today there is on both sides of a really common cause less of the sand of controversy and more of the dust of digging.

Of course, a racial motive remains—legitimately compatible with scientific method and aim. The work our race students now regard as important, they undertake very naturally to overcome in part certain handicaps of disparagement and omission too well known to particularize. But they do so not merely that we may not wrongfully be deprived of the spiritual nourishment of our cultural past, but also that the full story of human collaboration and interdependence may be told and realized. Especially is this likely to be the effect of the latest and most fascinating of all of the attempts to open up the closed Negro past, namely, the important study of African cultural origins and sources. The bigotry of civiliza-

---

* Arthur A. Shomburg, "The Negro Digs Up His Past," *An Anthology of American Negro Literature,* edited by Sylvestre C. Watkins (New York: The Modern Library, 1944), pp. 101-107.

tion, which is the taproot of intellectual prejudice, begins far back and must be corrected at its source. Fundamentally, it has come about from that depreciation of Africa which has sprung up from ignorance of her true rôle and position in human history and the early development of culture. The Negro has been a man without a history because he has been considered a man without a worthy culture. But a new notion of the cultural attainment and potentialities of the African stocks has recently come about, partly through the corrective influence of the more scientific study of African institutions and early cultural history, partly through growing appreciation of the skill and beauty, and in many cases, the historical priority of the African native crafts, and finally, through the signal recognition which first in France and Germany but now very generally, the astonishing art of the African sculptures has received. Into these fascinating new vistas, with limited horizons lifting in all directions, the mind of the Negro has leapt forward faster than the slow clearings of scholarship will yet safely permit. But there is no doubt that here is a field full of the most intriguing and inspiring possibilities. Already the Negro sees himself against a reclaimed background, in a perspective that will give pride and self-respect ample scope, and make history yield for him the same values that the treasured past of any people affords.

— Reading No. 6 —

THE UNIVERSAL ETHIOPIAN
ANTHEM, 1920*

At the 1920 convention in New York over which Marcus Garvey presided, Article 40 of the "Declaration of Rights of the Negro Peoples" resolved that "Ethiopia, Thou Land of Our Fathers" should be the "anthem of the Negro race."

✓   ✓   ✓

* Raymond Leslie Buell, *The Native Problem in Africa*, 2 vols. (New York: The Macmillan Company, 1928), Vol. II, pp. 969-970.

(Poem by Burrell and Ford)

I.

Ethiopia, thou land of our fathers,
Thou land where the gods loved to be,
As storm cloud at night suddenly gathers
Our armies come rushing to thee.
We must in the fight be victorious
When swords are thrust outward to gleam;
For us will the vict'ry be glorious
When led by the red, black and green.

CHORUS

Advance, advance to victory,
Let Africa be free;
Advance to meet the foe
With the might
Of the red, the black and the green.

II.

Ethiopia, the tyrant's falling,
Who smote thee upon thy knees,
And thy children are lustily calling
From over the distant seas.
Jehovah, the Great One, has heard us,
Has noted our sighs and our tears,
With His spirit of Love He has stirred us
To be One through the coming years.

CHORUS—Advance, advance, etc.

III.

O, Jehovah, thou God of the ages,
Grant unto our sons that lead
The wisdom Thou gave to Thy sages,
When Israel was sore in need.
Thy voice thro' the dim past has spoken,
Ethiopia shall stretch forth her hand,
By Thee shall all fetters be broken,
And Heav'n bless our dear fatherland.

CHORUS—Advance, advance, etc.

— Reading No. 7 —

THE FIRST PAN-AFRICAN
CONGRESS, 1919*

The first Pan-African Congress, held in Paris in 1919, announced goals that would be considered modest by present standards. No mention is made of African unity, and the request for self-government is couched in terms of gradualism.

✓   ✓   ✓

The resolutions of the Congress asked in part:

A. That the Allied and Associated Powers establish a code of law for the international protection of the natives of Africa, similar to the proposed international code for labor.

B. That the League of Nations establish a permanent Bureau charged with the special duty of overseeing the application of these laws to the political, social, and economic welfare of the natives.

C. The Negroes of the world demand that hereafter the natives of Africa and the peoples of African descent be governed according to the following principles:

1. *The land:* the land and its natural resources shall be held in trust for the natives and at all times they shall have effective ownership of as much land as they can profitably develop.

2. *Capital:* the investment of capital and granting of concessions shall be so regulated as to prevent the exploitation of the natives and the exhaustion of the natural wealth of the country. Concessions shall always be limited in time and subject to State control. The growing social needs of the natives must be regarded and the profits taxed for social and material benefit of the natives.

3. *Labor:* slavery and corporal punishment shall be abolished and forced labor except in punishment for crime; and the general conditions of labor shall be prescribed and regulated by the State.

4. *Education:* it shall be the right of every native child to learn to read and write his own language, and the lan-

* W. E. Burghardt Du Bois, *The World and Africa* (New York: The Viking Press, 1947), pp. 11-12.

guage of the trustee nation, at public expense, and to be given technical instruction in some branch of industry. The State shall also educate as large a number of natives as possible in higher technical and cultural training and maintain a corps of native teachers.

5. *The State:* the natives of Africa must have the right to participate in the government as fast as their development permits, in conformity with the principle that the government exists for the natives, and not the natives for the government. They shall at once be allowed to participate in local and tribal government, according to ancient usage, and this participation shall gradually extend, as education and experience proceed, to the higher offices of State; to the end that, in time, Africa be ruled by consent of the Africans. . . . Whenever it is proven that African natives are not receiving just treatment at the hands of any State or that any State deliberately excludes its civilized citizens or subjects of Negro descent from its body politic and cultural, it shall be the duty of the League of Nations to bring the matter to the notice of the civilized World.

— Reading No. 8 —

"ODE TO STOOLS AND STOOL WORSHIP" *

"A nation's tower of strength in time of need!" is what K. Macneill Stewart, a West Indian living in Ghana, calls ancestral, kingly stools. "In yon mute things repose a nation's soul."

ɟ   ɟ   ɟ

Temple of souls! symbolic shrine of rest!
    Mysterious relic of the dead and slain;
        Where dwell the spirits of a vanished reign
Of gods or men: where no vain tread molest
    Or ever can disturb the host that sleep

* *African Affairs,* Vol. 52, No. 208, July 1953 (*Journal of the Royal African Society*), pp. 185-187.

In you mute tomb where mourners do not weep,
And there's no place for such dull things as tears,
In dismal haunts of ancient cults and fears!

Then senses sicken and unnerve the mind,
    High-tensioned by an all-absorbing awe!—
    The cob-webbed walls, the dust-encumbered floor:
The stifling atmosphere with breath unkind:
    The narrow room with light-dimmed, crumbling folds,
    Where ghosts dance in a ghost-like dance that holds
The human conscience in a grip that aches,
As though caught in the coils of phantom snakes!

Here rest the Stools!—their sides lean to the wall:
    On these once sat some bold, despotic king:
    Each Stool a moving, living, vital thing;
Amidst a scene where, viewless, hangs a pall:
    In yon mute things repose a nation's soul,—
    Its power and the means of its control
Over all men and things: Stools never die—
Nor age, though endless centuries flicker by!

The nation finds religion centred, here;
    In the grim room of Stools a faith is born,
    Ancestral worship through the Stools, adorn,
These cults of centuries glossed with a veneer,
    Incomprehensible and mysterious;
    In parts repellent—yet so marvellous,—
These rites and customs of another age—
The glory of a people's heritage!

From whence these mystic cults!—Egypt or Tyre!
    Chaldea or the hot plains of Araby!
    These Stools! these rites! these customs!—can it be,
That these things pregnant with celestial fire,
    Hold forth a quenchless torch in silent praise
    Of mighty Africa's forgotten days!
A time that was—and is no more!—an hour,
When Africa wielded imperial power!

Mysterious, ever-conscious Continent!
    The lamb is slain! What now avails the feast
    Of gods or spirits! What invokes the priest!
What hot libation! What enthused content
    Surge through the breast of mortals standing round
    Yon reddened spot—the sacred blood-tipped ground!
What grand burnt-offering simmers on yon fire,
That wakes wild passions and a strong desire!

These moving customs are as old as man!
    These mystic rituals of Africa,
    That seem to emanate from countries, far,
Removed from where the actual race began!
    This self-same choice for sacred things—the sheep:
    The sacrifice—So moving and so deep!
Was Africa with Genesis! From where
Came the resemblance in these customs, here!

Abraham, Moses, David—Jesus, too,
    Followed a course of conduct that we know,
    That influenced man in every clime, below!
It seems that Ethiopia, also, knew
    The God-head and its grand philosophy:
    The meaning of the soul—Eternity:
A something after death, to understand
Man's timeless journey in that weary land!

No man is buried, here, just as he died!
    He is prepared as one about to go
    On some long journey; and the things we know
He needs are got for him. The great Divide,
    Has its own place in Africa's deep mind,
    With meaning similar to all mankind;
As proof, customs, religions—all are one;
And customs are by man, in time, undone!

Here, faith, religion, centres in one thing—
    The Stool: take this away—the nation dies
    And even colour fades out of the skies
Of Africa. All aspirations spring
    From this sole fount: hence these mysterious rites;
    And forms of worship, passions and delights:
The sacrifices, picturesque, austere:
The invocations and intensive prayer!

It is not to a soulless thing of wood,
    This ritual is done! this dance and feast!—
    This hot libation poured by some aged priest!
The gifts of wine and sacrificial food,
    Are for the souls that dwell within the Stool
    Of dead ancestors, true to cult and rule:
It is a faith, immutable—a creed;
A nation's tower of strength in time of need!

The Pharaoh sleeping in some buried place
    Of dismal earth where desert poppies grow,
    And where the chilly winds of centuries blow,
Once felt the happy thrill and joy of race;

The pride and glory of the things that be;
        The feel of power—the might of victory!—
In the same way, in Africa, great kings,
Felt transports in these transitory things.

These mystic rites—these Stools can never fade!
        They are too wonderful and too profound!
        Too much a part of being!—where men have found
More than a faith . . . And he was wise who made
        All mortal things—and things immortal, too:
        The mighty sun—the smallest bell of dew;
Each with its own impassioned mystery,—
A burning secret—and a destiny!

— Reading No. 9 —

"THE PARABLE OF THE EAGLE"*

After spending a score of years teaching in a small North Carolina college, Dr. James Aggrey returned to Africa and soon became a leading light at the newly founded and subsequently influential Achimota College in the Gold Coast. Known for his statement that both black and white keys are necessary to play the piano, he sought harmonization of the races. In parables such as these he sought to instil self-respect during the formative years of African nationalism.

↗   ↗   ↗

A certain man went through a forest seeking any bird of interest he might find. He caught a young eagle, brought it home and put it among his fowls and ducks and turkeys, and gave it chickens' food to eat even though it was an eagle, the king of birds.

Five years later a naturalist came to see him and, after passing through his garden, said: 'That bird is an eagle, not a chicken.'

'Yes,' said its owner, 'but I have trained it to be a chicken.

* Reprinted with permission of the publishers, Drum Publications (Proprietary) Limited and The Faith Press Ltd.

It is no longer an eagle, it is a chicken, even though it measures fifteen feet from tip to tip of its wings.'

'No,' said the naturalist, 'it is an eagle still: it has the heart of an eagle, and I will make it soar high up to the heavens.'

'No,' said the owner, 'it is a chicken, and it will never fly.'

They agreed to test it. The naturalist picked up the eagle, held it up, and said with great intensity: 'Eagle, thou art an eagle; thou dost belong to the sky and not to this earth; stretch forth thy wings and fly.'

The eagle turned this way and that, and then, looking down, saw the chickens eating their food, and down he jumped.

The owner said: 'I told you it was a chicken.'

'No,' said the naturalist, 'it is an eagle. Give it another chance to-morrow.'

So the next day he took it to the top of the house and said: 'Eagle, thou art an eagle; stretch forth thy wings and fly.' But again the eagle, seeing the chickens feeding, jumped down and fed with them.

Then the owner said: 'I told you it was a chicken.'

'No,' asserted the naturalist, 'it is an eagle, and it still has the heart of an eagle; only give it one more chance, and I will make it fly to-morrow.'

The next morning he rose early and took the eagle outside the city, away from the houses, to the foot of a high mountain. The sun was just rising, gilding the top of the mountain with gold, and every crag was glistening in the joy of that beautiful morning.

He picked up the eagle and said to it: 'Eagle, thou art an eagle; thou dost belong to the sky and not to this earth; stretch forth thy wings and fly!'

The eagle looked around and trembled as if new life were coming to it; but it did not fly. The naturalist then made it look straight at the sun. Suddenly it stretched out its wings and, with the screech of an eagle, it mounted higher and higher and never returned. It was an eagle, though it had been kept and tamed as a chicken!

My people of Africa, we were created in the image of God, but men have made us think that we are chickens, and we still think we are; but we are eagles. Stretch forth your wings and fly! Don't be content with the food of chickens!

— Reading No. 10 —

"NKRUMAISM WILL TRIUMPH," 1962*

Undertaking the simultaneous goals of unifying a nation, building it up economically, and unifying a continent was bound to bring opposition to "Africa's Man of Destiny," Kwame Nkrumah. The following editorial, written in flamboyant prose, came after a bomb attempt on his life.

✓ ✓ ✓

The rising tide of international reaction against Ghana reached its crescendo of turbulence during the month of September, towards the end of which the imperialist press and radio, on both sides of the Atlantic, actually circulated a most abominable lie about our beloved Life President of the Republic of Ghana, Osagyefo Dr. Kwame Nkrumah.

Incidents leading to the declaration of a state of Emergency in the Ghana capital and the harbour township of Tema have unmistakably exposed the existence of a global conspiracy against Ghana, manipulated by the agents of world imperialism and with the active collaboration of the reactionary section of the Western press.

Among the reasons which have so far been advanced for the desperate gamble by the organized forces of neo-colonialism to blunt the spearhead of the African Liberation Movement is the Ghana President's declaration earlier this year that IMPERIALISM MUST QUIT AFRICA BY THE END OF THIS YEAR OF GRACE, 1962.

At this stage, it is relevant to the Messianic Mission of Africa's Man of Destiny to restate some of the fundamental concepts of the Ghana Revolution, founded upon the ideological principles of Nkrumaism. In the first place, our dynamic Party represents the rank and file of all workers, farmers and progressive intellectuals.

On the domestic front, our Party stands for Freedom for all and for the progressive development of all States in continental Africa into a powerful nation utilising the boundless resources of our rich land for the benefit of her own peoples.

Internationally, our Party's policy is non-alignment and

* *The Party,* No. 25, September 1962 (Accra: Convention People's Party Bureau of Information and Publicity), p. 1.

positive neutralism, as has so often been stated by the Founder of the Nation himself. At the same time, we do not believe in passive neutrality when matters affecting the destiny of Africa are at stake. We are friends of all nations and the enemy of none.

These are the ramparts we defend. And it is this irrevocable stand for Nkrumaism which has been made the target of the whole might of the imperialists and their despicable African stooges.

Our inspired leader, Osagyefo Katamanto, Oyeadieyie, Kwame Nkrumah, who commands the unflinching loyalty and support of all the seven million inhabitants of this country, is proud to be paying at this time in his political career the price of courageous leadership.

But we are convinced of the justness of our Messiah's sacred mission to effectuate a United States of Africa. And our dynamic Party, under our time-tested leader, Teacher and Father has pledged itself to the remorseless prosecution of the battle against the crafty enemy.

In this crusade, we shall use every legitimate weapon in our armoury. We shall ask for no quarter or give any. We shall keep ever aloft the blazing torch of Nkrumaism until the crumbling ramparts of imperialism, colonialism and neo-colonialism are razed to the ground.

Nkrumaism shall triumph!
Long live Osagyefo!
Long Live Our Dynamic Party!
Long Live Ghana!

— Reading No. 11 —

CONSTITUTION OF THE CONVENTION PEOPLE'S PARTY OF THE GOLD COAST, 1950*

At the tenth anniversary of his coming to power in 1951 President Kwame Nkrumah of Ghana stated, ". . . the

* George Padmore, *The Gold Coast Revolution* (London: Dennis Dobson, Ltd., 1953), pp. 254-255.

Party makes the Government." Having been created by him, the Convention People's Party (C.P.P.) clearly reflects his personality.

✓   ✓   ✓

NAME

The Party shall be known and called the Convention People's Party.

AIMS AND OBJECTS (NATIONAL)

(I) SELF-GOVERNMENT NOW and the development of (Gold Coast) Ghana on the basis of Socialism.

(II) To fight relentlessly to achieve and maintain independence for the people of (Gold Coast) Ghana and their chiefs.

(III) To serve as the vigorous conscious political vanguard for removing all forms of oppression and for the establishment of a democratic socialist society.

(IV) To secure and maintain the complete unity of the Colony, Ashanti, Northern Territories and Trans-Volta.

(V) To work with and in the interest of the Trade Union Movement, and other kindred organizations, in joint political or other action in harmony with the Constitution and Standing Orders of the Party.

(VI) To work for a speedy reconstruction of a better (Gold Coast) Ghana in which the people and their chiefs shall have the right to live and govern themselves as free people.

(VII) To promote the Political, Social and Economic emancipation of the people, more particularly of those who depend directly upon their own exertions by hand or by brain for the means of life.

(VIII) To establish a Socialist State in which all men and women shall have equal opportunity and where there shall be no capitalist exploitation.

AIMS AND OBJECTS (INTERNATIONAL)

(I) To work with other nationalist democratic and socialist movements in Africa and other continents, with a view to abolishing imperialism, colonialism, racialism, tribalism and all forms of national and racial oppression and economic inequality among nations, races and peoples and to support all action for world peace.

(II) To support the demand for a West African Federation and of Pan-Africanism by promoting unity of action among the peoples of Africa and African descent.

— Reading No. 12 —

PASSIVE RESISTANCE IN SOUTH AFRICA, 1952*

This simple and eloquent plaint as quoted in "The Bantu World," November 15, 1952, was read in court to the Bloemfontein magistrate during the passive resistance campaign of 1952.

✓   ✓   ✓

We have decided voluntarily, and without any form of compulsion having been exerted upon us, to defy the laws which not only we non-Europeans regard as extremely unjust, but also a growing number of Europeans in this country.

It has been suggested by our European administrators, Your Worship included, that we should ventilate our grievances through the "proper channels," and that, as it is now, the law needs must take its course against us. Some there are who have even gone so far as to suggest that, as these laws were passed by Parliament, we should see to it that the same Parliament repealed or amended them. You will be the first to agree, Your Worship, that we have exhausted all attempts to air our genuine sufferings through the so-called "proper channels."

The history of our struggle for liberation is a sad story of unfulfilled or broken promises by our White administrators. It is a history characterized by obsequious representations and cap-in-hand deputations. The Natives' Representative Council was a "proper channel"—albeit an ineffective one—through which we could draw the attention of the Government to our sorry lot. The Council is now no more. The Location Advisory Boards and the Bungas, toy telephones

---

* Leo Kuper, *Passive Resistance in South Africa* (New Haven: Yale University Press, 1957), pp. 128-131.

that they actually are, are also some of the oft-spoken "proper channels."

Theirs is an ineffectual voice. Our so-called European Native representatives in Parliament are yet other "proper channels." These representatives were the first to admit that theirs was a voice in the wilderness as they were battling against "a stone wall of colour prejudice" in Parliament. Is there any wonder therefore that we have decided to throw caution to the winds—in so far as personal consequences are concerned—and embark upon this painful method of airing our grievances? To suggest that we should bring pressure to bear upon Parliament to repeal or amend these unjust laws is to make mockery of our sufferings. It is common knowledge that, because of our colour, we are a voteless and voiceless majority.

It is interesting to speculate, Your Worship, what the reaction of the European would be, were he, just by sheer miracle, to discover himself an African just overnight and thus be subjected to the thousand and one irksome discriminatory laws that our people have borne for centuries with Christian-like fortitude. This I say, because just recently two South African Members of Parliament protested strongly against alleged discrimination, real or imaginary, to which, so they said, they were subjected in India; discrimination which by mere comparison with what is our daily dose of this satanic doctrine is not worthy of the name. And, to come nearer home, Europeans are up in arms in South Africa against the introduction of the population registration measure which they regard as the extension of the pass system to them.

The local curfew regulation which is one of our targets of defiance is extremely unfair. Hitherto, our movements in town were limited up to 10 p.m. But recently the Minister of Native Affairs, with the approval of the City Council, brought down the time to 9 p.m., and this notwithstanding the protestations of the "proper channel," the local Native Advisory Board, that is. The majority of trains leave the station long after 9 p.m., and many an African man or woman has been arrested for the "crime" of having gone to see somebody off at the station after 9 p.m.

It has been our painful observation that, whenever apartheid is practised, we are always the sufferers. The endless queues at the ticket office during public holidays or weekends, and the equally long queues in the local post office, will convince any one that it is being taken as a matter of course that we must ever be satisfied with unequal and inadequate facilities.

Even in a location that is supposed to be our own; in a

location where we are left "to develop along our own lines," we have no freedom whatever. Your parent, wife or relative needs must get a permit before he can sojourn with you. Indeed, Your Worship, when you stop to think how painful, how humiliating some of these restrictions are to people that are living in a supposedly free and democratic country, the wonder will not be that we have embarked upon this resistance campaign at all, but that it has taken us so long a time to do so.

We do not quarrel with Your Worship when you say you have no alternative but to punish us for deliberately breaking the unjust laws; that is the unenviable duty you are bound to carry out. But, with due respect to Your Worship, we wish to state that punishment, no matter how severe, can be no deterrent to us. We have undertaken this campaign fully expecting such punishment. We have steeled and braced ourselves up to bear whatever punishment may come our way. And, happily, we derive encouragement and inspiration from the knowledge that practically the whole of the African population in Bloemfontein is four-square behind us, if not actively, then at least morally.

— Reading No. 13 —

THE PRICE OF FREEDOM, SHARPEVILLE, SOUTH AFRICA, 1960*

The following description of the massacre at Sharpeville, South Africa on March 21, 1960 was written by Susan Mamaki Mohanoe, Assistant Branch Secretary of the Pan Africanist Congress of South Africa.

✓   ✓   ✓

On 19th December 1959 my organization, the Pan-Africanist Congress, at its annual national conference held at Orlando, Johannesburg, resolved to embark upon a campaign directed against the Pass Laws which subject the African people to the humiliation of constant arrests. We, as an organization concerned with the rights and freedom of our people, felt we could no longer tolerate the persecution of these arrests and gaol confinement and therefore set a date upon which we would call upon the people to support us when we surrendered ourselves for arrest in protest and in an attempt to have the Pass Laws repealed.

I might mention, too, that the other aims and objects of our Pan Africanist Organization are:—The inculcation of Nationalism in our people and the pursuance of a struggle to achieve complete freedom from foreign domination and the oppression and exploitation which go together with rule by foreigners; the creation of African trade unions and their right to recognition; a minimum wage for all Africans of thirty-five pounds ($98) a month.

Our slogan for the anti-pass campaign is: *No Bail; No Defense; No Fine* . . . that is none of those participating in the anti-Pass campaign would bail themselves whilst awaiting trial for the inevitable arrests . . . no defense upon their being charged and tried and when sentence is passed . . . no fines were to be paid where the alternative for payment of fines were permitted.

During the week before 20th March 1960, we wrote to the Vereeniging Town Clerk, requesting for permission to hold a public meeting on that Sunday; an abrupt reply emanating from this office was received by us, arbitrarily refusing us the right to address any gathering. The campaign against the Passes was to commence on Monday 21st March. Having failed to hold a public meeting, we called upon our members to meet at the Sharpeville Tennis Court grounds (Sharpeville is the African location at Vereeniging).

At 1 a.m. of 21st, a great number of people had assembled at the tennis court where we addressed them on the objects of the campaign and announced to them our decision to commence with our planned campaign to surrender ourselves peacefully to the police for arrest that day. At 1.30 a.m. a Riot Squad lorry together with two Security Staff Cars arrived at the scene of the meeting; and without endeavoring to ask anybody what the gathering was about, the police started shooting from their vehicles into the air in order to frighten and disperse the crowd. In the confusion the police proceeded to attack us by baton charge, lashing out indiscriminately and causing many injuries. Among those injured were our Vice-Chairman and Secretary. There were about 50 police involved in this attack and, being heavily armed, they caused the people to seek sanctuary in retreat.

Towards dawn a great number of armed White police invaded the location and whilst they were ostensibly patrolling the streets, intimidated people with the obvious intention of causing retaliation so that they might be afforded an excuse to carry out their object of smashing by brutal force the opposition to the Pass Laws. Notwithstanding the police behavior, the people evinced no desire to go to work since they had by now decided to engage themselves in the campaign which we were going to start that day. The people stood waiting at street corners and bus termini, shouting slogans that they were no longer going to carry passes in support of our campaign.

When the leaders of the Pan Africanist Congress came marching from their homes towards the police station where, in accordance with their decision, they were going to surrender themselves for arrest, crowds followed them rhyming *Izwe Lethu—I Afrika—Our Land—Africa*—to the tune of the alternate National Anthem—*Nkosi Sikelela I Afrika*. This was an orderly crowd that marched towards the police station, loud, true, but loud with happiness that at last something was being done to deliver them from the tyranny of the notorious Pass Laws. The Vice Chairman and the Secretary of the P.A.C. led the people who now formed a long procession and, arriving at the police station, informed the police sergeant that they had come to surrender themselves for arrest as they were not in possession of their Passes. When the people heard this statement being voiced, they spontaneously and unanimously indicated that they too were surrendering themselves for arrest in support of the leaders. The White police sergeant evidently considered the situation to be beyond him and requested the leaders to wait for the police commander, who would, he said, be coming later. The leaders in turn asked the large crowd to wait outside the police station for the arrival of this officer. At about 10 a.m. the Commander arrived and was informed that the two leaders had come to surrender themselves for arrest as a protest against the Pass Laws, whereupon he exploded with anger and shouted "Vandag klop ons julle donder kaffers" (Today we'll thrash you kaffirs); half an hour later five Riot Squad lorries arrived packed with White police who were armed to the teeth with machine guns, Sten guns and pistols . . . they were followed by ten Saracen tanks with guns exposed and these were parked facing the crowd which surrounded the fence of the police station. *"Izwe Lethu—Afrika!"* chanted the people and, as people of Africa will always do, they stood to attention, singing *Nkosi Sikelela I Afrika (God Bless Africa)* whilst the police arrogantly displayed their power. The military too, of the Government, moved in and the Air Force planes droned above us and with a syntony that madness sometimes acquires there was being prepared the most monstrous of criminal acts against the African people. Our

Secretary, who had as yet not been locked up, asked me to find him an aspirin for his headache; I took this to him, and as I was turning back to the crowd, a bulky white man in civilian clothes shouted "Skiet die donner Kaffer meid" (Shoot the d... kaffir maid) when, all of a sudden, pandemonium was let loose. I heard screams, cries of anguish, and the showers of death had been let loose on men, women, and children.

As I attempted to escape, I tripped and fell, somebody fell on top of me. I could feel whimpers of agony above me. The body above me was ominously silent. Was death on me? How much can a human being go through with that thought? I endeavored to move away and managed to slip gently from the person on top of me. Then realizing I was alive and in danger, started to run away from the noise to seek refuge from this macabre reality. Upon reaching houses and safety, and recovering my wits, I obtained writing material in order to take down the names of the injured people. I observed that ambulances, private lorries, and cars, were engaged in collecting bodies . . . the injured to hospitals and the dead unceremoniously thrown into the police garage. At this stage I was one of the spectators who saw the insane brutality of the White police. I saw them pick up a tiny boy and throw him up in the air, allowing the body to fall of its own motion to the ground. I later saw the face of that child and it cannot have been more than ten years old and he was dead. The 21st of March 1960 was a day of stark and criminal massacre of African lives . . . Score for Verwoerd over 70 dead and hundreds injured. For the African . . . 70 widows, widowers and orphans . . . the price of Apartheid . . . the costly and inevitable price that we have to pay for Freedom.

— Reading No. 14 —

THE CULTURAL CONTRIBUTIONS AND PROSPECTS OF AFRICA*

Cheikh Anta Diop, a Senegalese, has written widely on the African cultural scene. The following talk was given at The First International Conference of Negro Writers and Artists in Paris, 1956.

↗   ↗   ↗

Ladies and Gentlemen,

I am going to talk to you to-night, first about the contribution of Negro Africa to civilisation, secondly about the cultural prospects of Africa, and in the third place about the specific nature of African culture. You will therefore see that the Paper for which I am responsible is an extremely complicated technical Paper which it has been almost impossible to prepare in full.

An important idea has been expressed by our comrade Césaire, and referred to again by the last speaker, namely the idea of a people of craftsmen; it is obvious that it is the people who create the basis of the tradition, but it is the elite who draw upon it to create the higher forms of culture.

This remark alone justifies the perspectives which I will try to draw here.

In general, writers start from artistic considerations in assessing what mankind owes to the Negro world in its slow progress through the ages. This is a way of restricting the problem at the outset, of limiting it to the single field of feeling. This unconsciously partial attitude is the result of a historical and social context which we cannot elaborate here. How should the problem be put? It seemed to us more judicious to make the effort to re-discover the general history of the Negro world and that of the African world in particular. Starting from this knowledge of our past, it becomes possible to assess the African contribution to the progress of the world by a simple process of comparison, beginning with

* Cheikh Anta Diop, "The Cultural Contributions and Prospects of Africa," *The First International Conference of Negro Writers and Artists* (Paris: Presence Africaine, Vol. XVIII-XIX, 1956), pp. 349-354.

the fundamental features of African culture and taking chronology into account.

Embarking upon these researches led to the discovery, beyond all doubt, that the ancient Egyptian and Pharaonic civilisation was a Negro civilisation. From this point of view arguments have been adduced both anthropological, ethnological, linguistic, historical and cultural. To judge their value it is enough to refer to the work *Nations Nègres et Culture*, published by *Présence Africaine*. If need be these arguments will be recalled to the members of Congress during discussions in the Commissions with a view to drawing up the Final Report which will be published.

However, if time allows, I will try to give a few examples.

It is important to make one major point clear straight away. If Egyptian civilisation was Negro, that does not mean that all the Negroes now living on the continent took part in it in the same degree. It is true that round about Egypt and the Meroitic Sudan (formerly called the Anglo-Egyptian Sudan) which were already civilised in the days of Diodorus Siculus, there existed African tribes which "did not yet know humanity" (the expression comes from Diodorus himself) which were in all probability real savages roaming round the Nile Valley like the Barbarians of our IV century round the Roman Empire. They were the Xyllophages (eaters of grasshoppers), Strutophages (eaters of ostriches), as the Greeks called them, the Ichtyophages (fish eaters) and those whom Diodorus calls "the drivers of elephants." Perhaps this explains to a certain extent the different level of culture which is found in certain African peoples, leaving aside the retrogression due to re-tribalisation provoked by colonialism. This latter factor is often predominant in explaining the backward state of certain tribes.

It remains none the less true that the Egyptian experiment was essentially Negro, and that all Africans can draw the same moral advantage from it that Westerners draw from Graeco-Latin civilisation.

At present it becomes relatively easy to assess the contribution of the Negro towards human progress. As one might foresee, it will go beyond the traditional limits of art.

In so far as Egypt was incontestably the great initiator of the Mediterranean world, this contribution exists in the fields of science, architecture, philosophy, music, religion, literature, art and social life etc. . . . I cannot here stress the detail of this vast influence which embraces all branches of activity since the beginning of time. There is all the less reason to do this since the fact is not challenged by any specialist. The specialists are merely content to look for an extra-African, White, origin for Egyptian civilisation.

It has been enough for us to demonstrate in a fashion which can hardly be contested, the Negro origin of Egyptian Pharaonic civilisation to determine by that fact alone the Negro contribution to human progress. In discussion it will therefore be possible to criticise very closely the idea of a Negro Egypt. And here I would like to cite you a few examples.

Herodotus was an Indo-European; he therefore had no interest in asserting that "the Egyptians had dark skin and curly hair," that they were Negroes and that it was they who had civilised the Mediterranean world, if it was not true. One can no longer doubt the value of these arguments; if it was a question of analysing complex facts, facts of a social nature, or some other nature, it might have been possible to cast doubt on them, but one must at least admit that a traveller who arrives in a country is capable of recognising the colour of the inhabitants' skin. And it is merely an observation of this kind which Herodotus makes.

His evidence has been found to be correct on much more complex questions.

In the fifth century B.C. an island of Negroes, the Colchians, lived on the Shores of the Black Sea; their origin interested all the scholars of antiquity. Herodotus suggests an explanation in his Book II: "The Egyptians did, however, say that they thought the original Colchians were men from Sesostris' army. My own idea on the subject was based first on the fact that they have black skins and woolly hair"; he gives other reasons upon which I will not dwell. It is certain that Herodotus' opinion about the origin of the Egyptians is not an isolated one. All the scholars and writers of antiquity bore witness in the same sense, Diodorus Siculus, Strabo, Aeschylus etc, etc.

When Herodotus employs the root "melanos," the strongest word which existed in Greek to describe a Negro, modern scholars translate by "bronzed skin, sunburnt skin." But let justice be done; there are some scholars of good faith. I will give you proof. A member of the Institute travelled in Egypt between 1783 and 1785, I refer to Volney, the famous scholar Volney. The revelations which he made after his voyage in the Near East caused a sensation, and here is his testimony about the Egyptian people after 5,000 years of history; "They all have puffy faces, protruding eyes, flat noses and thick lips, in other words a real mulatto face. I was tempted to attribute it to the climate, until after visiting the Sphinx, its appearance gave me the clue to the puzzle. On seeing that head, so characteristic of the Negro in all its features, I remembered that remarkable passage of Herodotus where he says 'For my part I think the Colchians are a colony of the Egyptians, because like them, they have black skins and woolly hair', that is that the ancient Egyptians were real Negroes like all the natives of Africa, and that explains why their blood, mingled for many centuries with that of the Greeks and Romans, must have lost the intensity of its original colouring while retaining the imprint of its pristine mould. One can even give this preliminary observation a very general scope and raise the question that physiognomy is a sort of monument which is appropriate in many cases to establish or throw light upon the origins of peoples etc." Further on Volney concludes, "But, reverting to Egypt, the facts which she has contributed to history afford many reflections to the philosopher. What a subject for meditation to see the present barbarism and ignorance of the Copts issued from the alliance of the profound genius of the Egyptians and the brilliant spirit of the Greeks, and to think that this black race which is to-day our slave and the object of our despising is the one to which we owe our arts and sciences and even the use of language. Imagine finally that it is in the midst of people who claim to be the friends of liberty and humanity that sanction has been given to the most barbarous slavery and the question has been raised whether Negroes have an intelligence of the same kind as White men." (Volney, *Voyages en Syrie et en Egypte,* Paris 1787, Vol. I, pp. 74-77).

Champollion discovered to his surprise that in 1500 B.C., according to the Egyptian bas-reliefs, the white race was the most savage of all mankind and was at the bottom of the scale, whereas the Egyptians and the Sudanese (Nubians) were at the head of civilisation. At the sight of these paintings he cried. "But the sight of them nevertheless has something flattering and consoling, since it enables us properly to appreciate the road we have since travelled." (Cf: Letter 13, cited in *Nations Nègres*).

Another Egyptologist of good faith, Amélineau, does not express himself differently. From his study of Egyptian civilisation, Amélineau arrived at the following conclusion; "The conclusion which flows from these considerations is that the conquered people of the Anous initiated these conquerors into at least a part of the road of civilisation and art, and this conclusion, it will easily be seen, is one of the most important for the history of human civilisation, and consequently of religion. Egyptian civilisation—this is perfectly clear from what has gone before—is not of Asiatic origin, but of African origin, of Negroid origin, however paradoxical this assertion may seem. We are not accustomed to endowing the Negro race and the neighbouring races with intelligence, with enough intelligence even to have been able to make the first discoveries necessary for civilisation; there is, however, no single one of the tribes now inhabiting the interior of Africa which has not possessed, which does not still possess one or other of these first discoveries etc." (Cf. *Nations Nègres*.)

In re-discovering our past in this way we have contrived to re-create that historical consciousness without which there can be no great nation. [Italics added.]

Let us now turn to the other cultural prospects of Africa. It is essential to specify the background against which we place ourselves in speaking of culture. This conception, to my mind, is linked with the emergence of a multi-national State embracing practically the whole of the Continent. That is to say that the cultural problems will only arise in their full force on the day when we have achieved national independence on the continental scale by a victorious struggle against colonialism. Certainly, in the course of this struggle cultural weapons are already necessary; no-one can do without them. That is why we must forge them in parallel within the framework of our struggle for national independence. Culture will therefore be essentially at the service of the fight for national liberation.

When we have created, as I have just said, a continental and multi-national sovereign State, it must be endowed, whatever one may say, with an ideological and cultural superstructure which will be one of the essential bulwarks of security. That means that this State, as a whole, must be conscious of its past, which implies the preparation of a General History of the Continent, embracing the individual histories of the different nationalities. The role of history in the life of a people is sufficiently well known to make it unnecessary to stress it here. One of our preoccupations has been to work out the broad lines of this History of the Continent. If we ponder for a few instants on the plane of artistic creation, we see that it is not valid, that it does not reflect the national soul of a people except so far as the artist has drawn upon the sources of Tradition, that is, so far as he is not really cut off from his Past, even if he is creating in reaction against it.

But the real basis of culture is language. Many African intellectuals are impotent in face of the difficulties raised by the African linguistic mosaic. They forget that the fact is general, and not peculiar to Africa. They forget that Africa is a Continent and not a single Nation and that there is no continent in the world where linguistic unity has been achieved. To remind ourselves of this, let us cite the linguistic mosaic of India which is only a fraction of the Asiatic continent; or of Europe where more than a hundred languages and dialects are spoken, which does not prevent Europeans from communicating with each other. In effect, these languages are not all situated on the same level, some are more important than others because of their extent, their wealth or the development of their literature, and above all because of the importance of the political role played by the countries where they are spoken. Thus in Europe to-day, instead of dreaming of establishing a common European language, in which even basic culture would be given to citizens of different nationalities, men are, in general, content to learn three languages, French, English and German, which enable them to make themselves understood anywhere on the continent.

It would, nevertheless, be possible to choose an African language which would become a governmental language. We do not, however, disguise the difficulties which that presents; they will certainly be raised in the course of discussion, but they will not be any greater in the Africa of the future than those which the Government of India is now encountering in imposing Hindi. It is astonishing to see that India has not accepted the accomplished fact, that is a linguistic unity achieved on the national scale—at any rate in appearance —but on the basis of a foreign language, English being the official language during the colonial period. It would therefore have seemed convenient to use it to drown the 300 native languages and dialects. But the Indian authorities, who are not wanting in profundity, realised that it did not come to the same thing to impose a native or a foreign language on the people. The latter implies a cultural alienation out of all proportion with the cultural alienation implied in extending a native language to the whole group. In other words an Italian is less alienated culturally when French is imposed upon him than if a Zulu language were imposed upon him. That is what the Indian authorities saw clearly, and in the face of this inevitable dilemma they have chosen the lesser evil.

The achievement of linguistic unity, whatever may be the historical background in which it is contemplated, always involves a certain alienation of small linguistic groups. But this fact is without importance if it is looked at closely; such minorities are always bilingual, and their second language is one of culture and expansion. It is for analogous reasons that, starting from the Ile de France, French has imposed itself upon the Basques, the Bretons and the Alsatians, for national reasons superior to the human reasons which would militate in favour of maintaining linguistic mosaic and anarchy. There are cases in which it is salutary to stifle dialects in order to stifle micro-nationalism. All peoples who have become great Nations have had to face this problem and have solved it.

The practical side of adopting a native form of expression can be demonstrated at all levels; it is easy to see that a French peasant would have no interest in allowing his son to be educated in the English language. The time needed to acquire the knowledge essential to agriculture, to health, in short to every citizen of a modern State would be at least doubled by the handicaps caused by the use of a foreign form of expression. In the same line of thought, if we want to educate the average African, we shall be obliged to resort to a native form of expression.

Certainly this reform cannot be introduced overnight. There is no question of pressing for the immediate creation of vernacular schools. We should be handicapped by the absence of qualified teachers and appropriate text books and by the lack of technical terms in existing languages. But the need nevertheless remains. Nothing could equal the value of such an experiment in revivifying the national soul of a people.

Thus it is the duty of African intellectuals to harness themselves to the solution of the problems which will have to be settled if this revolution is to be achieved at the earliest desirable moment. Along these lines some work has been done in clearing the ground partly by studying in detail the kinship of the African languages, establishing their individual genius, and studying grammatical aspects which have hitherto been disregarded by the experts and partly by integrating technical terms on the basis of judicious conventions. (Cf. *Nations Nègres.*)

I now come to the problem of Art. It has been very frequently discussed in the course of this Congress, and therefore I will not dwell upon it.

I will merely say that Art as a whole, that is, sculpture, painting, music and architecture, should help the African to realise himself more and more each day. The majesty of its rhythms and accents should be on the scale of the continent.

One might have analysed American music and pointed out the profound kinship in the realm of feeling which exists between it and African music, and then what is lacking to make it, for example, an African national music; American music was born in such special conditions that the coefficient of national pride in it is comparatively low; that is why it could not be the basis of an African national music. In the realm of feeling there is a Negro kinship which all of us can feel. Thus American music is effectively Negro music, but it cannot be a national music.

The last prospect for contemplation is the industrial prospect.

You will very well remember that I was supposed to bring

out the prospects for the future, and I was therefore supposed on the level of history, of language, of culture in general and of technical and industrial organisation to advocate valid and virtually acceptable proposals. That is responsible for the heterogeneous character of my Paper. Very well, Industrial Prospects.

They are perhaps the most important, because they must be realised first so that we may all the better achieve the others. It is by industrialisation to the utmost that we shall obtain the material power necessary to guarantee our political frontiers, pending the establishment of that planetary unity which is so much talked of.

In this field Nature has not overlooked Negro Africa. Our continent is, so to speak, the centre of the world's energy and raw materials. In the face of our reserves of hydraulic energy, of uranium and thorium, of solar, aeolian and tidal energy and so forth and of the raw materials of the equatorial zone, not to speak of other minerals, Europe is like an empty cupboard compared with Africa. This idea is so obvious that instead of continuing to enlarge its industrial infrastructure, Europe finds it now more advantageous to build factories in Africa itself in proximity to the sources of energy and the raw materials. It has gone as far as contemplating the construction of equatorial barrages and the export of electrical energy to Europe by cable, thus obviating the need to push the industrialisation of the African continent to excess.

All this makes it easy to see clearly the industrial destiny of Africa and the need for her sons to equip themselves for the tasks which await them. *I urgently refer the reader to the article called "Alerte sous les Tropiques" which I published in the December-January 1956 number of the review "Présence Africaine."*

This article is a brief survey of African technical and industrial problems seen by an African. All comrades who are interested in the technical aspect of our problems should read it and meditate upon it.

In conclusion, upon the historical plane we know where we come from and it is true that you do not know where you are going until you know where you have come from. The problem of our antiquities is settled in its broad lines; we know the background against which we must work, the framework within which we must assemble facts to fill the gaps in our history, to create an African historical consciousness. On the linguistic plane we can say that an over easy solution is to be avoided and that it is necessary at all costs to elevate certain native languages to the level of modern requirements and make them capable of reflecting philosophic and scientific thought. On the plane of art it is necessary that the rhythm and majesty of art should be on the continental scale, that they should translate the pride of a people who are proud of their past and of themselves. On the industrial plane we are the centre of the world's energy, and that is the capital thing. It is no good talking of the fraternisation of peoples, of planetary unity, one can foresee that there will be a certain lapse of time before this comes about, because there are still many obscure forces existing in society. Therefore, more than ever it is necessary to be vigilant until such time as our energies can be employed in creating a material force which will enable us to guarantee our political frontiers on the basis of industrialisation to the utmost, founded on our sources of energy and our raw materials.

I should like to end by emphasizing a final capital prospect. While Negro Africa is orienting itself towards a multi-national State which will embrace practically the whole of the Continent with a first class industrial equipment, the Antilles could orient themselves towards the formation of a federation of islands on the lines of Indonesia, which instead of looking to America or Europe would maintain relations of fraternity and kinship, economic, commercial, cultural and political relations, with Negro Africa.

— Reading No. 15 —

CULTURE AND COLONISATION, 1956*

Aimé Césaire's poem "Cahiers d'un retour au pays natal" when re-published in 1947 is said to have introduced Négritude to a receptive group in Paris. Born in Martinique in 1913, Césaire illustrates the trans-Atlantic pull. The following is excerpted from his paper delivered to the First International Conference of Negro Writers and Artists.

✓   ✓   ✓

For the past few days we have been greatly exercised as regards the significance of this Congress.

* Aimé Césaire, "Culture and Colonisation," *First International Conference of Negro Writers and Artists* (Paris: Presence Africaine, Vol. XVIII-XIX, 1956), pp. 193-207.

More particularly, we have wondered what is the common denominator of an assembly that can unite men as different as Africans of native Africa, and North Americans, as men from the West Indies and from Madagascar.

To my way of thinking the answer is obvious and may be briefly stated in the words: colonial situation. . . .

I think it is very true that culture must be national. It is, however, self-evident that national cultures, however differentiated they may be, are grouped by affinities. Moreover, these great cultural relationships, these great cultural families, have a name: they are called *civilisations*. In other words, if it is an undoubted fact that there is a French national culture, an Italian, English, Spanish, German, Russian, etc., national culture, it is no less evident that all these cultures, alongside genuine differences, show a certain number of striking similarities so that, though we can speak of national cultures peculiar to each of the countries mentioned above, we can equally well speak of a European civilisation.

In the same way we can speak of a large family of African cultures which collectively deserve the name of negro-African culture and which individually reveal the different cultures proper to each country of Africa. And we know that the hazards of history have caused the domain of this civilisation, the locus of this civilisation to exceed widely the boundaries of Africa. It is in this sense, therefore, that we may say that there are, if not centres, at least fringes of this negro-African civilisation in Brazil and in the West Indies, in Haiti and the French Antilles and even in the United States. . . .

This, I submit, is what legitimises our present meeting. All who have met here are united by a double solidarity; on the one hand, a *horizontal solidarity*, that is, a solidarity created for us by the colonial, semi-colonial or para-colonial situation imposed upon us from without; and on the other, a vertical solidarity, a *solidarity in time,* due to the fact that we started from an original unity, the unity of African civilisation, which has become diversified into a whole series of cultures all of which, in varying degrees, owe something to that civilisation.

But, it may be said, there is still another possibility, namely, the elaboration of a new civilisation, a civilisation that will owe something both to Europe and to the native civilisation. If we discard the two solutions represented, on the one hand, by the preservation of the native civilisation and, on the other, by the export overseas of the colonists' civilisation, might it not be possible to conceive of a process that would elaborate a new civilisation owing full allegiance to neither of its component parts?

This is an illusion cherished by many Europeans who imagine they are witnessing in countries of British or French colonisation the birth of an Anglo- or Franco-African or an Anglo- or Franco-Asiatic civilisation.

In support of it they rely on the notion that all civilisations live by borrowing, and infer that when two different civilisations have been brought into contact through colonisation, the native civilisation will borrow cultural elements from the colonists' civilisation and that from this marriage will spring a new civilisation, a mixed civilisation.

The error inherent in such a theory is that it reposes on the illusion that colonisation is a contact with civilisation like any other and that all borrowings are equally good.

The truth is quite otherwise and the borrowing is only valid when it is counter-balanced by an interior state of mind that *calls* for it and integrates it within the body which then assimilates it so that both become one—what was external becoming internal. . . .

Colonisation is a different case. Here there is no borrowing arising out of need, no cultural elements being spontaneously integrated within the subject's world. And Malinowski and his school are right to insist that the process of cultural contact must be regarded mainly as a continuous process of interaction between groups having different cultures.

What does this mean if not that the colonial situation, that sets the colonist and the colonised in opposing camps, is in the last resort the determining element?

And what is the result?

The result of this lack of integration by the dialectic of need is the existence in all colonial countries of what can only be termed a cultural mosaic. By this I mean that in all colonial countries the cultural features are juxtaposed but not harmonised. . . .

"Culture is above all a unity of artistic style in all the vital manifestations of a people. To know many things and to have learnt much are neither an essential step towards culture nor a sign of culture and could indeed go hand in hand with the opposite of culture, namely, barbarism, *which implies a lack of style or a chaotic mixture of all styles*" [*Nietschze*].

No truer description could be given of the cultural situation common to all colonised countries. In every colonised country we note that the harmonious synthesis of the old native culture has been destroyed and has been replaced by a heterogeneous mixture of features taken from different cultures, jostling one another but not harmonising. This is not necessarily barbarism through lack of culture. *It is barbarism through cultural anarchy.* . . .

But, it may be asked, once the original unity is broken, is it not possible that the colonised people can reconstitute it and integrate its new experiences, hence its new wealth, with the framework of a new unity, a unity that will not, of course, be the old unity, but a unity nevertheless?

Agreed. But it must be realized that such a solution is impossible under the colonial system because such a mingling, such a commingling, cannot be expected from a people unless that people retains the *historic initiative,* in other terms, unless that people is free. Which is incompatible with colonialism. . . .

Thus the cultural position in colonial countries is tragic. Wherever colonisation occurs, native culture begins to wither. And among the ruins there springs up, not a culture, but a kind of sub-culture, a sub-culture that, because it is condemned to remain marginal as regards the European culture and to be the province of a small group, an "élite," living in artificial conditions and deprived of life-giving contact with the masses and with popular culture, is thus prevented from blossoming into a true culture.

The result is the creation of vast stretches of cultural wastelands or, what amounts to the same thing, of cultural perversion or cultural by-products.

This is the situation which we black men of culture must have the courage to face squarely.

The question then arises: in such a situation, what ought we, what can we, do? Clearly our responsibilities are grave. What can we do? The problem is often summarised as a choice to be made. A choice between native tradition and European civilisation. Either to reject native civilisation as puerile, inadequate, outdated by history, or else, in order to preserve our native cultural heritage, to barricade ourselves against European civilisation and reject it.

In other terms, we are called upon to choose: "Choose between fidelity and backwardness, or progress and renunciation."

What is our reply?

Our reply is that things are not as simple as they seem and that the choice offered is not a valid one. Life (I say life and not abstract thought) does not recognise, does not accept these alternatives. Or rather if these alternatives are offered, life itself will transcend them.

We say that the question does not arise in native society alone, that in every society there is always a state of equilibrium between old and new, that it is always precarious, that it is in a constant state of readjustment and that it has in practice to be rediscovered by every generation.

Our societies, our civilisations, our native cultures are not exempt from this law.

For our part, and as regards our particular societies, we believe that in the African culture yet to be born, or in the para-African culture yet to be born, there will be many new elements, modern elements, elements, let us face it, borrowed from Europe. But we also believe that many traditional elements will persist in these cultures. We refuse to yield to the temptation of the *tabula rasa*. I refuse to believe that the future African culture can totally and brutally reject the former African culture. . . .

I believe that the civilisation that has given negro sculpture to the world of art; that the civilisation that has given to the political and social world the original communal institutions such as village democracy, or fraternal age-groups, or family property, which is a negation of capitalism, or so many institutions bearing the imprint of the spirit of solidarity; that this civilisation that, on another plane, has given to the moral world an original philosophy based on respect for life and integration within the cosmos; I refuse to believe that this civilisation, imperfect though it may be, must be annihilated or denied as a pre-condition of the renaissance of the native peoples.

I believe that, once the external obstacles have been overcome, our particular cultures contain within them enough strength, enough vitality, enough regenerative powers to adapt themselves to the conditions of the modern world and that they will prove able to provide for all political, social, economic or cultural problems, valid and original solutions, that will be *valid because they are original*.

In the culture that is yet to be born, there will be without any doubt both old and new. Which new elements? Which old? Here alone our ignorance begins. And in truth it is not for the individual to reply. Only the community can give the answer. We may, however, affirm here and now that *it will be given* and not verbally but by facts and by action.

And this is what finally enables us to define our role as black men of culture. Our role is not to prepare *a priori* the plan of future native culture, to predict which elements will be integrated and which rejected. Our role, an infinitely more humble one, is to proclaim the coming and prepare the way for those who hold the answer—the people, our peoples, freed from their shackles, our peoples with their creative genius finally freed from all that impedes them and renders them sterile.

To-day we are in a cultural chaos. Our part is to say: "Free the demiurge that alone can organise this chaos into a new synthesis, a synthesis that will deserve the name of culture, a synthesis that will be a reconciliation and an overstepping of both old and new." We are here to ask, nay to demand: "Let the peoples speak! Let the black peoples take their place upon the great stage of history!"

— Reading No. 16 —

"THE SPIRIT OF CIVILISATION, OR THE LAWS OF AFRICAN NEGRO CULTURE" *

The following excerpts are taken from a subtle paper given at The First Conference of Negro Writers and Artists in 1956 by the dean of African men of letters, Leopold Senghor, now President of the Republic of Senegal.

ↆ ↆ ↆ

Whether we like it or not, 1955 will mark an important date in the history of the world, and first and foremost in the history of the coloured peoples. Bandoeng will be from now on a rallying for these peoples. . . . How can we believe that the Bandoeng spirit, which for us is primarily a spirit of culture, does not also animate the Indians, and particularly the Negroes of America? For the Negro race, more than any other, was the victim of the great discoveries. The European Renaissance was built on the ruins of African Negro civilisation, the force of America has waxed fat on Negro blood and sweat. The slave trade cost Africa two hundred million dead. But who can tell what cultural wealth was lost? By the grace of God, the flame is not quenched, the leaven is still there in our wounded hearts and bodies to make possible our Renaissance to-day.

But this Renaissance will be the doing not so much of the

* Leopold Sedar Senghor, "The Spirit of Civilisation, or the Laws of African Negro Culture," *The First Conference of Negro Writers and Artists* (Paris: Presence Africaine, 1956), pp. 51-64.

politicians, as of the Negro writers and artists. Experience has proved it, cultural liberation is an essential condition of political liberation. If white America conceded the claims of the Negroes it will be because writers and artists, by showing the true visage of the race, have restored its dignity; if Europe is beginning to reckon with Africa, it is because her traditional sculpture, music, dancing, literature and philosophy are henceforth forced upon an astonished world. This means that if the Negro Writers and artists of to-day want to finish off the work in the Bandoeng spirit they must go to school in Negro Africa. Gide already noted at the beginning of the century that, for an artist or writer, the most effective way of being appreciated and understood by the stranger is still to nourish his work from the roots of his own soil.

There can be no question in this introduction to our Cultural Stocktaking of getting lost in detail, or even dealing with the different literary and artistic forms. There is no question of making a survey of African Negro civilisation, but rather of culture, which is the spirit of civilisation. We must . . . first of all sketch out a physio-psychology of the Negro.

It has often been said that the Negro is the man of Nature. By tradition he lives of the soil and with the soil, in and by the Cosmos. He is sensual, a being with open senses, with no intermediary between subject and object, himself at once the subject and the object. He is, first of all, sounds, scents, rhythms, forms and colours; I would say that he is touch, before being eye like the White European. He feels more than he sees; he feels himself. It is in himself, in his own flesh, that he receives and feels the radiations which emanate from every existing object. Stimulated, he responds to the call, and abandons himself, going from subject to object, from Me to Thee on the vibrations of the Other: he is not assimilated: he assimilates himself with the other, which is the best road to knowledge.

This means that the Negro by tradition is not devoid of reason, as I am supposed to have said. But his reason is not discursive: it is synthetic. It is not antagonistic: it is sympathetic. It is another form of knowledge. The Negro reason does not impoverish things, it does not mould them into rigid patterns by eliminating the roots and the sap: it flows in the arteries of things, it weds all their contours to dwell at the living heart of the real. White reason is analytic through utilisation: Negro reason is intuitive through participation.

This indicates the sensitiveness of the coloured man, his emotional power. Gobineau defines the Negro as "the being

who is most energetically affected by artistic emotion." For
what affects the Negro is not so much the appearance of an
object as its profound reality, its super-reality; not so much
its form as its meaning. Water moves him because it flows,
fluid and blue, above all because it cleanses, still more because it purifies. Form and meaning express the same
ambivalent reality. Emphasis is nevertheless laid on the
meaning, which is the signification of the real, no longer
utilitarian, but moral and mystic, a symbol. It is not without
interest that contemporary scholars themselves assert the
primacy of intuitive knowledge by "sympathy." "The finest
emotion we can experience is mystic emotion. There lies the
seed of all art and all real science."

It is this physio-psychology of the Negro which explains
his metaphysics, and therefore his social life, of which literature and art are only one aspect. For social life in Negro
Africa rests, according to Father Placide Tempels, on a
combination of logically co-ordinated and motivated concepts. Those whom the Europeans call "primitives," asserts
the same missionary, "live" more than the Europeans do, "by
ideas and according to their ideas."

At the centre of the system, animating it as the sun animates our world, is existence, that is, life. This is the supreme
good, and the whole activity of man is directed solely
towards the increase and expression of vital power. The
Negro identifies being with life, or, more specifically, with
vital force. His metaphysics is an existential ontology. As
Father Tempels writes, "being is that which has force," or
better, "being is force." But this force is not static. Being is
in unstable equilibrium, always capable of gaining or losing
force. In order to exist, man must realize his individual essence by the increase and expression of his vital force. But
his force, the sub-stratum of intellectual and moral life, and
to that extent immortal, is not really living and cannot really
grow except by co-existing in man with the body and the
breath of life. These, being made of substance, are perishable,
and disintegrate after death.

But man is not the only being in the world. A vital force
similar to his own animates every object which is endowed
with a sentient character, from God to a grain of Sand. The
Negro has drawn up a rigid hierarchy of Forces. At the summit, a single God, uncreated and creator, "He who has force
and power of himself. He gives being, substance and increase
to the other forces." After him come the ancestors, and first,
the founders of clans, the "demi-gods." Then, going down
the scale, we come to the living, who are, in their turn,
ordered according to custom, but above all in order of

primogeniture. Finally, at the bottom of the scale, the classes of animals, vegetables, minerals. Within each other the same hierarchy.

This is the appropriate place to point out the outstanding place occupied by Man at the centre of this system, in his quality of a person, actively existing, capable of increasing his being. For the universe is a closed system of forces, individual and distinct it is true, but unified. Thus all creation is centred on man. To the extent that the being is a vital force, the ancestors, if they do not wish to be non-existent, "perfectly dead"—it is a Bantu expression—must devote themselves to reinforcing life and existence, which enables them to share in it. As for the inferior beings—animals, vegetables, minerals—they have no other purpose in the designs of God, except to support the actions of the dead. They are instruments, not ends in themselves.

The merit of this existential ontology is that it has, in its own turn, inspired a harmonious civilisation. And in the first place, an authentic religion. For what is a religion, if not, as its etymology indicates, the link which gives the universe its unity, which unites God to the lyme grass and the grain of sand?

This ontology is its dogma. With regard to cult, which is religion in act, in Negro Africa it is expressed by the sacrifice.

It is the head of the family who offers the sacrifice. He is the priest designated purely by his character as the eldest descendant of the common Ancestor. He is the natural mediator between the living and the dead. Nearer to the dead, he lives in intimacy with them. His flesh is less flesh, his spirit is less chained, his world more powerfully persuasive: he already shares the character of the dead. Sacrifice is, above all, an entering into relationship with the Ancestor, the dialogue of me and Thee. With him we share the nourishment whose existential force will give him the sentiment of life. And communion goes as far as identification, so that by an inverse movement the force of the Ancestor flows into the sacrificer and the community whom he incarnates. Sacrifice is the most typical illustration of the general law of the interaction of the vital forces of the Universe.

If we look at the natural aspects of society, the unit of order in the world, we find that the simplest component, the basic cellule is the family. African Negro society is, in effect, made up of widening concentric circles, superimposed and interlaced, formed on the pattern of the family. The tribe is a group of several families, the kingdom a group of several tribes. But what is the family? It is the clan, the totality of all those, living and dead, who recognize a common ancestor. This common ancestor is the link which

unites God to men and is himself a genie and a "demi-god."
His life often takes the form of a totemic myth, sometimes
linked with an astral myth. Hence the importance of the
animal in Negro cosmogony. The ancestor has received from
God a vital force, and his eternal vocation is to increase it.
We see that the aim of the family is to preserve in perpetuity
a patrimony of vital force which grows and intensifies itself
to the extent of which it is manifested in living bodies, in
more numerous and more prosperous human beings. The
family shows itself as a microcosm, an image of the universe,
which is reflected on an enlarged scale in the tribe and the
kingdom. The king is only the father of the greatest family;
he is the descendant of the Leader of Tribes.

The family, the tribe and the kingdom are not the only
communal organisations which at the same time bind and
sustain the Negro. Alongside them there is a whole network
of interlocking organisations. These are the *fraternities of
age,* a sort of friendly society to which a whole generation
belongs, the *craft guilds* and the *brotherhoods of secret rites.*
The latter have a social and political, or even religious, rôle.
In truth, all these organisations have a religious basis, among
peoples where the distinction between sacred and profane,
political and social, appears late and infrequently.

It is in social activities, sustained by religious feeling, that
literature and art naturally integrate themselves. A western
man finds it difficult to appreciate the place which social
activities, including literature and art, occupy in the African
Negro calendar. They are not relegated to Sundays or "the-
atrical evenings" but, to take the example of the Sudan Zone,
they fill the whole eight months of the dry season. At this
time men are fully occupied with their relations with the
Others: genies, ancestors, members of the family, the tribe,
the kingdom, even strangers. There are festivals all the time
and Death itself is the occasion for a festival, the supreme
Festival: festival of harvest and festival of sowing, births,
initiations, marriages, funerals: guild festivals and brotherhood festivals. And every evening, the vigil round the
hearth, with the leaping flames shining on tales, dances and
songs, gymnastic games, drama and comedy. Work itself,
which celebrates the marriage of Man and Earth is a narrative and a poem. Thus we have the songs of labour, the
songs of the peasant, the boatman, the herdsman. For in
Negro Africa, as we shall see, all literature and all art is
poetry.

The question all the time is to enter into relations either
with the legendary totemic Ancestors, or with the mythical
genies—but the genie is often merged with a star or an
animal, and the legend deepens into a myth. Significant in

this connexion is the festival of initiation, which is opened and accompanied by numerous sacrifices. It is concerned with initiation into the cosmogonic myth, the legends and customs of the tribe: more specifically with the birth of Knowledge through poetry, song, drama, and masked dance, to the primordial rhythm of the tom-tom. Then it is that the seed dies in order to germinate, that the child dies to himself, in order to be born again as an adult in the Initiator and the Ancestor. This is a religious, animistic existentialism. The other—Adult, Ancestor, genie or God—far from being an obstacle, is the supporter and the source of vital force. Far from there being any conflict in the confrontation of Me and Thee, there is a conciliatory agreement, not a de-realisation, but a greater realisation of the individual essence.

Literature and art are therefore not divorced from the generic activities of man, and particularly from skill in craftsmanship. They are its most effective expression. Do you remember in "The Negro Child" Laye's father forging a golden jewel? The prayer, or rather the poem, which he re-cites, the song of praise which the Griot sings as he works the gold, the dance of the smith at the end of the operation, it is all that—poem, song, dance—which, more than the gestures of the craftsman, accomplishes the work, and makes it into a work of art. The arts in the general sense of the word are, in the same perspective, linked together. Thus, sculpture only fully realises its object by the grace of the dance and the sung poem. Look at the man who incarnates Nyamié, the Sun-Genie of Baoulé, under the mask of the Ram. Watch him dancing the actions of a ram to the rhythm of the orchestra, while the chorus sings the poem of the deeds of the genie. In both cases we have a functional art. In this last example the masked dancer must identify himself with the Genie-Sun-Ram, and, like the sacrificer, com-municate his force to the audience which takes part in the drama.

This brings out another characteristic of the poem—once again. I call every work of art a poem; it is created by all and for all. True there are professional literary men and artists; in the Sudanese lands they are the Griots who are at the same time historiographers, poets and tellers of tales: in the lands of the Guinea and the Congo they are the civil Sculp-tors of the princely courts whose ermine epaulette is a badge of honour: everywhere they are the Smiths, as the multiple technicians of magic and art, the first artist, according to a Dogon myth, who, to the rhythm of the tom-tom made the rain fall. But alongside these professionals there is the peo-ple, the anonymous crowd which sings, dances, carves and paints. Initiation is the school of Negro Africa in which man, putting away childish things, assimilates, with the science of his tribe, the technique of literature and art. It will, moreover, be seen from the two examples given that every manifestation of art is collective, made for all, with the participation of all.

Because they are functional and collective, African Negro Literature and art are committed. That is their third general characteristic. They commit the person—and not only the individual—by and through the community, in the sense that they are techniques of essentialisation. They commit him to a future which will henceforth be to him the present, an essential part of his ego. That is why the African Negro works of art are not, as has often been said, copies of an archetype repeated a thousand times. Certainly there are subjects, each of which expresses a vital force. But what is striking is the variety of execution according to personal temperament and circumstances. Once again the craftsman-poet takes up his position, and commits, with himself, his race, his history and his geography. He makes use of the material which lies to his hand, and the daily facts which compose the weft of his life, while he scorns the anecdote, because, being without significance, it does not commit. Painter or sculptor, he will on occasion make use of instruments and materials imported from Europe: he will not hesitate to represent the machine, the pride of the West: he will go so far as to dress some ancestral genie in European style. In the new Society inspired by the spirit of the Colonial Pact, the teller of tales will not hesitate to give Money its due place, the leading one, as the incarnation of Evil. Because he is committed, the craftsman-poet is not concerned to create for eternity. Works of art are perishable. While their spirit and style are preserved, we hasten to replace the ancient work by modernising it as soon as it becomes out of date or perishes. This means that in Negro Africa "art for art's sake" does not exist; all art is social. The Griot who sings the noble to war makes him stronger and shares in the victory. When he hymns the deeds of a legendary hero, it is the history of his people which he writes with his words, by restoring to them the divine profundity of a myth. Right down to the fables, which, through tears and laughter, help to teach us. Through the dialectic which they express they are one of the essential factors in social equilibrium in the guise of the Lion, the Elephant, the Hyena, the Crocodile, the Hare, the Old Woman, we read clearly with our ears, our social structure and our passions—the good and bad alike. Sometimes it is the refusal, addressed to the Great Ones, the Right opposed to brute force. Sometimes it is acquiescence in the order of the universe of the

Ancestors and of God. And, concludes the Jolof, "thus the
fable threw itself into the sea. He who shall breathe it first
will go to Paradise." The savour of Negro wisdom! . . .

At the same time, it is impossible to seize the essence of
African Negro literature and art if one imagines that they
are purely utilitarian and that the African Negro has no
sense of beauty. Some ethnologists and art critics have gone
so far as to allege that the words "beauty" and "beautiful"
are missing from the African Negro Languages. The truth
is that the African Negro assimilates beauty to goodness,
and especially to effectiveness. Thus in the Jolof of Senegal,
the words târ and rafet, beauty and beautiful are more appropriate in referring to a person. In speaking of a work of
art Jolof would use the adjectives dyêka, yem, mat, which I
should translate by "fitting," "adequate," "perfect." Once
again, it is a question of functional beauty. A beautiful mask,
a beautiful poem, is one which produces in the public the
emotion aimed at: sadness, joy, hilarity, terror. The word
bahai—pronounced "bahhaï"—is significant. It means "goodness" and is used by the young dandies to describe an attractive young girl. Beauty for them is "the promise of
happiness." Conversely, a good deed is often called "beautiful."

If a given poem produces its effect, that is because it finds
an echo in the minds and feelings of its hearers. That is why
the Fulah define a poem as "words pleasing to the heart and
the ear." But if for the African Negro, as for the European,
"the great rule is to please," they do not both find pleasure
in the same things. In the Graeco-Latin aesthetic which
survived in the European West, except for the Middle Ages,
down to the end of the XIX century, art is the imitation of
Nature; I mean, of course, "adjusted imitation": in Negro
Africa, it is the explanation and knowledge of the world,
that is a sentient participation in reality which subtends the
universe towards super-reality, or more exactly towards the
vital forces which animate the universe. The European takes
pleasure in recognizing the world through the reproduction
of the object, which is called the "subject," the African Negro
from knowing it vitally through image and rhythm. With the
European the chords of the senses lead to the heart and the
head, with the African Negro to the heart and the belly, the
very root of life. The mask of the Ram gives pleasure to the
Baoulé spectators because it incarnates the sun-Genie in
plastic and rhythmic language.

Image and rhythm, these are the two fundamental features
of African Negro style.

Image first of all. But before going any further, we must
pause a moment on the question of language, so as to reach

an understanding of its nature and function from a brief study of the African Negro tongues. We shall thus be better able to appreciate the value of the African Negro image. . . .

The first outstanding characteristic of the African Negro languages is the wealth of their vocabulary. There are ten, and sometimes twenty words to describe an object, according as it changes form, weight, volume or colour; as many words to describe an action, according as it is simple or multiple, weak or strong, beginning or ending. In Fulah the nouns are divided into twenty-one genders, all neuter, under a classification based partly on their semantic value, partly on their phonetic value and partly on the grammatical category to which they belong. But it is the verb which remains most significant in this respect. In Jolof it is possible, by means of affixes, to construct from the same root more than twenty verbs with different shades of meaning, together with at least as many derivative nouns. Whereas current Indo-European languages lay emphasis on the abstract idea of time, the African Negro languages stress the aspect, the concrete fashion in which the verbal action unfolds itself. This means that they are essentially concrete languages. The words are always pregnant with images; through their value as signs transpires their value as sense.

The African Negro image is therefore not an equation-image, but an analogy-image, a surrealist image. The African Negro has a horror of the straight line and the false "right word." Two and two do not make four, but "five" in the words of the poet Aimé Césaire. The object does not signify what it represents, but what it suggests, what it creates. The elephant is strength, the spider, Prudence; horns are the Moon, and the moon is Fertility. Every representation is an image, and the image, I reiterate, is not an equation, but a symbol, an ideogramme. Not only a figure image, but substance—stone, earth, copper, gold, fibre—as well as line and colour. Any language is wearisome that does not tell a story. Better still, the African Negro does not understand such language. How astonished the first Whites were to discover that the "Natives" did not understand their pictures, or even the logic of their speeches.

I have spoken of a surrealistic image. But, as you might guess, African Negro surrealism is different from European surrealism. The European is empiric, the African is mystic and metaphysical. André Breton writes in *Signe ascendant*: "Poetic analogy"—by which we must understand European surrealist analogy—"differs fundamentally from mystic analogy in that it in no way presupposes, beyond the weft of the visible world, an invisible universe, which tends to manifest itself. It is entirely empiric in its approach." Negro surrealist analogy, on the other hand, presupposes and manifests the hierarchic universe of vital forces.

Power of the image, power of speech. So it is in Dahomey, among the *Fons,* where the king, on every outstanding occasion during his reign, uttered a rhythmic sentence, whose key word furnished a new name. "The *Pineapple* that laughed at the thunder." And the word, and the pineapple were despotically graven everywhere, and became an image: in wood, clay, gold, bronze and ivory; on the throne, the headgear, the commander's baton and the walls of the palace.

The proof is that in African Negro poetry the abstract word is rarely met with. Here there is no need to comment upon the image: the hearers are gifted with double vision. In sculpture some masks achieve an exemplary power of suggestion, such as the mask of the Genie-Moon-Bull among the Baoulé. A man's bearded face with the horns and ears of a bull—sometimes the horns are not a question of the anecdote or the "slice of life." The facts are images and have the value of examples. Hence the place of the recital, its progress by leaps and bounds, its material improbabilities, the absence of psychological explanation.

An image, however, does not achieve its effect with the African Negro unless it is rhythmic. Here the rhythm is consubstantial with the image; it is the rhythm which perfects the image by uniting sign and sense, flesh and spirit into one whole. It is only artificially and for the sake of a clearer account that I have distinguished the two elements. In the music which accompanies a poem or a dance the rhythm creates an image as much as the melody. In the mask of the Genie-Moon-Bull it is rhythm which makes it possible to substitute an image with the same symbolic value; crescent moon in place of horns and horn of abundance in place of birds.

What is rhythm? It is the architecture of the being, the internal dynamism which gives him form, the system of waves which he emits in relation to Others, the pure expression of vital force. Rhythm is the vibratory shock, the force which, through the senses, seizes us at the root of our being. It is expressed through the most material and most sensual means; lines, surfaces, colours and volumes in architecture, sculpture and painting: accents in poetry and music: but in doing this it guides all that is concrete towards the light of the mind. With the African Negro rhythm enlightens the spirit to the precise extent to which it is embodied in sensuality. African dancing abhors physical contact. But watch the dancers. If their lower limbs are shaken with the most sensual tremors, their heads are sharing in the serene beauty of the masks, of the Dead.

Once again, the primacy of Speech. It is rhythm which gives it its effective fulfillment, which changes it into the word. It is the word of God, that is, rhythmic speech, which created the world. It is also in the poem that we can best capture the nature of African Negro rhythm. In this case rhythm is not born of the alternation of long syllables and short syllables, but solely of the alternation of accented syllables and unaccented syllables, of strong tones and weak tones. The question is one of rhythmic versification. There is verse, and therefore a poem when an accented syllable recurs at the same interval of time. But the essential rhythm is not that of the words, but of the percussion instruments which accompany the human voice, and more specifically those of them which mark the basic rhythm. We are dealing with a multiple rhythm, a sort of rhythmic counterpoint. It is this which saves the words from that mechanical regularity which breeds monotony. In this way the poem appears as a piece of architecture, a mathematical formula based on unity in diversity. Here is the rhythm of the words in two Jolof poems chosen at random.

A) 24 00
24 00

44 00
44 00
43 00

43 00

B) 32 31
32 31

22 31
32 21

32 31
32 21

32 31
32 31

21 31

As may be guessed, the basic rhythm in the first case is 444, in the second 3333. In both cases the verse is a *tetrameter*. But the public often takes part in the poem. We then have two groups of rhythm; this allows both the leader of the reciters and the leader of the tom-toms to give themselves up entirely to their inspiration and to multiply countertime and syncope, solidly supported by the basic rhythm. For the monotonous basic rhythm, far from being a handicap to inspiration, is its essential condition. The rhythmic elements, however, are not limited to those which I have described. In addition to the clapping of the public and the steps and gesture of the reciters and the tambourinists, it should be noted that there are certain *figures of speech*—alliterations, paronomasis, anaphora—which, being based on the repetition of vocables or sounds form secondary rhythms and add to the effect of the whole. Finally, the poet makes ample use of those *descriptive words* whose importance has been brought out by M. de la Vergne de Tressan. He tells us that these words, formed by onomatopoeia sometimes amount to as much as a third of the vocabulary of African Negro languages.

The "prose recital" partakes of the grace of rhythm. In Negro Africa there is no fundamental difference between prose and poetry. Poetry is merely a more markedly and regularly rhythmic form of prose: it is recognized in practice from the fact that is is accompanied by a percussion instrument. The same phrase may become a poem by accentuating its rhythm, thus expressing the tension of being: the *being* of being. It appears that, "long, long ago" all recitals were strongly rhythmic, were poems. In more recent times the recital was still recited, and was spoken in a monotone voice and in a higher tone: it was an element in a religious ceremony. As we know it to-day even in the form of a fable, which is the most secularized form, it is still rhythmic, although not so strongly. In the first place *dramatic interest* is not spared, or more specifically, sparing the dramatic interest does not mean, as it does in modern European recitals, banishing repetition: quite the reverse, dramatic interest is created by repetition, the repetition of a fact, a gesture, a song or words which constitute a *leitmotiv*. But nearly always some new element is introduced, some variation in repetition, *a unity in diversity*. It is this new element which emphasizes the progress of the drama. This means that the prose recital is not above resorting both to figures of speech based on the repetition of vocables, and to descriptive words. That is not all: the structure of the African Negro sentence is naturally rhythmic. Because, whereas the Indo-European languages use a logical syntax of subordination, the African Negro languages turn more willingly to an intuitive syntax of co-ordination and juxtaposition. And, in propositions of almost equal length, the words are arranged in groups, which each have a major accent.

On the plane of rhythm, the music is linked to the words and the dance, but certainly more closely to the poem than to the dance. For the African Negro it is the element which specially characterizes the poems. In the Senegalese languages the same word—*woi* in Jolof, *kim* in Serer, *vimre* in Fulah—means the song and the supreme form of poem: the ode. In any event, a poem is not complete unless it is sung, or at any rate given rhythm by a musical instrument. And the prose of the public Crier is given solemnity and acquires authority by the voice of the tom-tom. It has often been observed that, in African Negro music, rhythm takes precedence over melody. This is because the object of music, as I have already said, is not so much to charm the ears as to *re-inforce* the words, to make them more effective. Hence the place which is given to rhythm, to sudden falls, inflexions and *vibrati;* hence the preference for *expression* over harmony.

Great stress has been laid in recent years on the ethnologic religious and social values of African Negro sculpture. And yet those writers and artists were not wrong who, at the beginning of the century emphasized its aesthetic value, its rhythm. Just look through the works which contain reproductions of African Negro sculpture, such as that of Carl Kjersmeier called *Style Centres of African Negro Sculpture* (Paris, Copenhagen). Pause over Figure 48, which represents a female statuette from *Baule.* Two themes of sweetness sing an antiphony. The ripe fruit of the breasts. The chin and the knees, the buttocks and the calves are also fruit or breasts. The neck, the arms, and the thighs are columns of black honey. In another volume this *Fang* statuette from Gaboon again offers us fruits—breasts, naval, knees—with which are contrasted the curved cylinders of the trunk the thighs and the calves. Now look in the first volume at this high *Bambara* mask, representing an antelope. Strophe of the horns and the ears; antistrophe of the tail and the neck and the hairs of a mane sprung from the sculptor's imagination. As André Malraux writes in *Les Voix du Silence;* "The African mask is not the fixation of a human expression, it is an apparition . . . The sculptor does not interpret the geometry of a phantom of which he is ignorant, he calls it up by his geometry: the effect of his mask comes not so much from the extent to which it is like a man, as from the extent to which it is unlike; the animal masks are not animals; the antelope mask is not an antelope, but the Antelope-Spirit, and it is its style which makes it a spirit." Its style must be understood to mean its rhythm.

Rhythm is even more manifest in African Negro painting. The modern painters of Potopoto and Elisabethville have begun to persuade attentive observers of this. They are merely following a tradition which is already ancient. We know that the African Negro sculptor is often a painter as well. And now, for the last twenty-five years, the mural paintings of Negro Africa have been discovered, reproduced and commented upon. In these paintings rhythm is not marked by dividing lines between light and shade; it is not *arabesque* as in classical European painting. African Negroes, for the rest, paint in flat colours, without shadow effects. Here as elsewhere, rhythm is born of the repetition, often at regular intervals, of a line, a colour, a figure, a geometric form, but above all from colour contrast. In general, against a dark ground, which creates the effect of space or dead time, and gives the picture its depth, the painter arranges his figures in light colours, or vice-versa. The design and colour of the figures correspond less to the appearance of reality than to the profound rhythm of the objects. . . .

I must come to an end. Such then is the African Negro for whom the world exists by the fact of its reflexion upon himself. He does not realise that he thinks: he feels that he feels, he feels his *existence,* he feels himself; and because he feels the Other, he is drawn towards the other, into the rhythm of the Other, to the re-born in knowledge of and of the world. Thus the act of knowledge is an "agreement of conciliation" with the world, the simultaneous consciousness and creation of the world in its indivisible unity. It is this urge of vital force which is expressed by the religious and social life of the African Negro, of which art and literature are the most effective instruments. And the poet sings: "Hail to the perfect circle of the world and ultimate concord!"

I shall be told that the spirit of the Civilisation and the laws of African Negro culture, as I have expounded them, are not peculiar to the African Negro, but are common to other peoples as well. I do not deny it. Each people unites in its own aspect the diverse features of mankind's condition. But I assert that these features will nowhere be found united in such equilibrium and such enlightenment, and that rhythm reigns nowhere so despotically. Nature has arranged things well in willing that each people, each race, each continent, should cultivate with special affection certain of the virtues of man; that is precisely where originality lies. And if it is also said that this African Negro culture resembles that of ancient Egypt, and of the Dravidian and Oceanic peoples like two sisters, I would answer that ancient Egypt was *African* and that Negro blood flows in imperious currents in the veins of the Dravidians and the Oceanics.

The spirit of African Negro civilisation consciously or not, animates the best Negro artists and writers of to-day, whether they come from Africa or America. So far as they are conscious of African Negro culture and are inspired by it they are elevated in the international scale; so far as they turn their backs on Africa the mother they degenerate and become feeble. Like Antaeus who needed to support himself on the earth in order to take flight towards the sky. That does not mean that the Negro artists and writers of to-day must turn their backs on reality and refuse to interpret the social realities of their background, their race, their nation, their class, far from it. We have seen that the spirit of African Negro civilisation became incarnate in the most day-to-day realities. But always it transcends these realities so as to express the meaning of the world.

The literary and artistic history of Europe proves that we should remain faithful to this spirit. After the set-back of Graeco-Roman aesthetics at the end of the XI century, the writers and artists of the West discovered Asia, and above all Africa, at the end of their quest. Thanks to Africa they were able to legitimate their discoveries by giving them a human value. This is not the moment that we should choose to betray, with Negro Africa, the very reason of our lives.

— Reading No. 17 —

TO NEW YORK*

Africa's leading intellectual, Leopold Sedar Senghor, has had an exceedingly full life as a professor in France, essayist, poet, political figure, and inspirer of a host of young Africans. Born in Senegal in 1906, he is now the President of the Republic. The following poem has been called "something like a manifesto of 'négritude.'"

✓   ✓   ✓

I

New York! At first I was confused by your beauty, by those
    great golden long-legged girls.
So shy at first before your metallic eyes, your frosted smile
So shy. And the anguish in the depths of sky-scraper streets
Lifting eyes hawkhooded to the sun's eclipse.
Sulphurous your light and livid the towers with heads that
    thunderbolt the sky

* Ulli Beier, "In Search of an African Personality," *The Twentieth Century*, Vol. CLXV, No. 986, April 1959, pp. 348-349.

The skyscrapers which defy the storms with muscles of steel
    and stone-glazed hide.
But two weeks on the bare sidewalks of Manhattan
—At the end of the third week the fever seizes you with the
    pounce of a leopard
Two weeks without rivers or fields, all the birds of the air
Falling sudden and dead on the high ashes of flat roof-tops.
No smile of a child blooms, his hand refreshed in my hand.
No mother's breast, but only nylon legs. Legs and breasts
    that have no sweat nor smell.
No tender word for there are no lips, only artificial hearts
    payed for in hard cash
And no book where wisdom may be read. The painter's
    palette blossoms with crystals of coral.
Nights of insomnia oh nights of Manhattan! So agitated by
    flickering lights, while motor horns howl of empty hours
And while dark waters carry away hygienic loves, like rivers
    flooded with the corpses of children.

II

Now is the time of signs and of reckonings
New York! Now is the time of manna and hyssop.
You must but listen to the trombones of God, let your heart
    beat in the rhythm of blood, your blood.
I saw in Harlem humming with noise with stately colours and
    flamboyant smells
—It was tea-time at the house of the seller of pharmaceutical
    products—
I saw preparing the festival of night for escape from the day.
    I proclaim night more truthful than the day.
It was the pure hour when in the streets God makes the life
    that goes back beyond memory spring up
All the amphibious elements shining like suns.
Harlem Harlem! Now I saw Harlem! A green breeze of corn
    springs up from the pavements ploughed by the naked
    feet of dancers
Bottoms waves of silk and sword blade breasts, water-lily
    ballets and fabulous masks.
At the feet of police horses roll the mangoes of love from
    low houses.
And I saw along the sidewalks streams of white run streams
    of black milk in the blue fog of cigars.
I saw the sky in the evening snow cotton-flowers and sera-
    phims wings and sorcerers plumes.
Listen New York! Oh listen to your male voice of brass
    vibrating with oboes, the anguish choked with tears fall-
    ing in great clots of blood
Listen to the distant beating of your nocturnal heart, rhythm
    and blood of the tom-tom, tom-tom blood and tom-tom.

THE CONTINENT THAT LIES WITHIN US

III

New York! I say to you: New York! let black blood flow
    into your blood

That it may rub the rust from your steel joints, like an oil
    of life

That it may give to your bridges the bend of buttocks and
    the suppleness of creepers.

Now return the most ancient times, the unity recovered, the
    reconciliation of the Lion, the Bull and the Tree

Thoughts linked to act, ear to heart, sign to sense.

There are your rivers murmuring with scented crocodiles
    and mirage-eyed manatees. And no need to invent the
    Sirens.

But it is enough to open the eyes to the rainbow of April

And the ears, above all the ears, to God who out of the laugh
    of a saxophone created the heaven and the earth in six
    days.

And the seventh day he slept the great sleep of the negro.

— Reading No. 18 —

THE CONTINENT THAT LIES WITHIN US *

*Holding a degree in medicine from Cambridge University,
and now Principal of Fourah Bay College in Sierra Leone,
Dr. Davidson Nicol has also written short stories and articles.
"You are not a country, Africa, you are a concept," he says
upon returning.*

Africa, you were once just a name to me,
But now you lie before me with sombre green challenge
To that loud faith of freedom (life more abundant)
Which we once professed, shouting
Into the silent, listening microphone;
Or, on a London platform, to a sea
Of white, perplexed faces, troubled

* *An Anthology of West African Verse*, compiled by Olembe
    Bassir (Ibadan: Ibadan University Press, 1957), pp. 63-
    66.

With secret Imperial doubt, shouting
Of you with a vision euphemistic
As you always appear
To your lonely sons in alien shores . . .
(Then in my wistful exile's mind
The dusty East End lane would vanish
In a grey mental mist, leaving behind
A warm, shimmering image of you.)

The hibiscus blooming in shameless scarlet,
And the bougainvillea in mauve passion
Entwining itself around strong branches;
The pal trees standing like tall, proud, moral women,
Shaking their plaited locks against
The cool, suggestive evening breeze;
The short twilight dwindling;
The white, full moon turning its round gladness
Towards the swept open space
Among the trees; there will be
Dancing there tonight, and in my brimming heart
Plenty love and plenty laughter.

Oh, I am tired of sausages and mash
With trifle and cream to follow,
Of clay-brown tea in breakfast cups,
And "Please return your trays here."

I am tired of grim-faced, black-coated men
Reading the *Financial Times* with impersonal fear,
Of slim City typists, picking their sandwich lunches
Like forlorn sparrows, in chromium milk bars;
Of unfulfilled men shouting the racing editions
As I buy my ticket to Camden Town, N.W.1.

I am tired of crouching over the spluttering gas fire
In this my lone bed-sitter;
Of queuing up for cheap lamb chops,
At two for one-and-three.

The only thing I am not tired of
Is the persistent kindness
Of you too few who are not afraid
Of my blank dusky strangeness.
But now I am back

Gazing at the sophistication of your brave new cities
Whose very names hold promise—
Dakar, Bathurst, Cotonou,
Lagos, Accra, and Bissau;
Monrovia, Freetown, Libreville,
Freetown is really in my mind.

Go up country, so they say,
To see the real Africa;
For whoever you may be,
That is where you come from;
Go for bush, inside the bush,
There you'll find your hidden heart,
Your mute, ancestral spirit.

And so I went, hopeful on my way.

    But now you lie before me, passive, actual
With your unanswering green challenge:
Is this all you are?
This long, uneven red road, this occasional succession
Of huddled heaps of four mud walls
And thatched falling grass roofs,
Sometimes ennobled by a thin layer
Of white plaster, and covered with dull, silvery,
Slanting, corrugated zinc.
Those patient faces on weather-beaten bodies
Bowing under heavy market loads.
The pedalling cyclist wavers by
On the wrong side of the road,
As if uncertain of this new emancipation.
The squawking chickens, the pregnant she-goats
Lumber awkwardly with fear across the road,
Across the windscreen view of my four-cylinder kit-car.
An overladen lorry speeds madly onwards,
Full of produce, passengers, with driver leaning
Out into the swirling dust to pilot his
Swinging, obsessed vehicle along.
Beside him on the raised seat his first-class
Passengers, clutching and timid, but he drives on
At so, so many miles per hour, peering out with
Bloodshot eyes, unshaven face and dedicated look:
His motto painted across—"Sunshine Transport,"
                                        "We get you

There, quick, quick." "The Lord is my Shepherd"—
(The red dust settles down on the green leaves).
I know I shall not want, my Lord,
Though I have reddened your green pastures,
It is only because I have wanted so much
That I have always been found wanting.
From South and East and from my West
(The sandy desert holds the North)
We have looked across a vast continent and
Dared to call it ours. You are not a country,
Africa, you are a concept, which we all

Fashion in our minds, each to each, to
Hide our separate years, to dream our separate dreams.
Only those within you who know their circumscribed
Plot, and till it well with steady plough
Can from that harvest then look up
To the vast blue inside of the enamelled bowl of sky,
Which covers you and say, "This is my Africa," meaning
"I am content and I am happy. I am fulfilled, within,
Without and roundabout. I have gained the little
Longings of my hands, my heart, my skin, and the soul
That follows in my shadow."
I know now that is what you are, Africa,
Happiness, contentment and fulfilment,
And a small bird singing on a mango tree.

— Reading No. 19 —

A MORNING IN THE HEART OF AFRICA*

The murder of Patrice Lumumba in early 1961 was one of the most dramatic events in a sequence of discord, confusion, violence, and bitterness as the former Belgian Congo attained independence. Here the Congo's first Premier, advocate of a unified Congo, expresses the emotions of millions of Africans.

For a thousand years you, Negro, suffered like a beast,
    your ashes strewn to the wind that roams the desert.

Your tyrants built the lustrous, magic temples
    to preserve your soul, preserve your suffering.
Barbaric right of fist and the white right to a whip,
    you had the right to die, you also could weep.

In your totem they carved endless hunger, endless bonds,
    and even in the cover of the woods a ghastly cruel death
    was watching, snaky, crawling to you like branches from
        the holes and heads of trees
    embraced your body and your ailing soul.

* Patrice Lumumba, "A Morning in the Heart of Africa," *Africa Today*. Vol. VIII, No. 2, February 1961, p. 2. (Reprinted from *Link,* India.)

Then they put a treacherous big viper on your chest,
    on your neck they laid the yoke of fire-water,
      they took your sweet wife for the glitter of cheap pearls,
    your incredible riches that nobody could measure.

From your hut, the tom-toms sounded into the dark of night
    carrying cruel laments up mighty black rivers
    about abused girls, streams of tears and blood,
      about ships that sailed to the country where the little man
    wallows in an ant-hill and where dollar is the king,
    to that damned land which they called a motherland.

There your child, your wife were ground day and night
    by frightful, merciless mill, crushing them in dreadful pain.

You are man like others. They preach you to believe
    that good white god will reconcile all men at last.

By fire you grieved and sang the moaning songs
    of homeless beggar that sings at strangers' doors.

And when a craze possessed you and your blood boiled through the night
    you danced, you moaned,
Like the fury of a storm to lyrics of a manly tune
    a strength burst out of you for a thousand years of misery
    in metallic voice of jazz, in uncovered outcry
    that thunders through the continent in gigantic surf.

The whole world, surprised, woke up in panic
    to the violent rhythm of blood, to the violent rhythm of jazz,
    the white man turning pallid over this new song
    that carries torch of purple through the dark of night.

The dawn is here, my brother, dawn! Look in our faces,
    a new morning breaks in our old Africa.

Ours only will now be the land, the water, the mighty rivers
    which the poor Negro was surrendering for a thousand years.

And hard torches of the sun will shine for us again
    they'll dry the tears in your eyes and the spittle on your face.

The moment when you break the chains, the heavy fetters,
    the evil, cruel times will go never to come again.

A free and gallant Congo will arise from the black soil,
    a free and gallant Congo—the black blossom, the black seed!

THE UNITY AND RESPONSIBILITIES OF NEGRO-AFRICAN CULTURE, 1956*

The first International Conference of Negro Writers and Artists held at the Sorbonne, September 19-22, 1956, provided a rich and interesting program of speeches and discussion. From it grew the Society of African Culture which herein sets the stage for the second conference (not held until 1959).

1   1   1

One of the resolutions of the first Conference of Negro Writers and Artists, which was held in Paris in 1956, has resulted in the birth of the Society of African Culture (S.A.C.). This association comprises men of culture of the Negro world, and its mission is to organize our cultural action in such a way that:

a) our culture patterns be first interpreted by ourselves.
b) that they express both our inner life in its very reality, and the universal vocation of our cultures.

The Society of African Culture is therefore carrying out its mission by organizing a second Conference in which the Negroes of culture representing its various national sections will participate: members of the American national Section (U.S.A.), those of the Haiti Republic, those of the different countries of Africa, etc. . . . .

Our first Conference in 1956 had for its central theme the crisis of Negro Culture. Our principal concern at that time was to point out the causes responsible for that crisis and to dissipate the ambiguous conceptions of Western nations which, through ignorance of the contribution of Afro-Asian peoples to mankind's heritage, and the conscious and systematic action exerted against indigenous cultures, has accepted the idea that there can be a nation without a culture of its own.

This year, our preoccupation is less critical and more con-

* "The First International Conference of Negro Writers and Artists," *Presence Africaine,* Vol. XVIII-XIX, 1956, pp. 11-12 of supplement.

structive in character. We are dealing with cultural unity and solidarity.

We are, of course, scattered over the face of the earth, as colonialism, slavery and racialism have flung us. We live under different political and economic regimes and we belong to different nations. We find ourselves in Arab, Portuguese, French, English, etc. . . . cultures which differ considerably from one another and form our traditional Negro Culture.

Yet, we have common features in our aspirations, in our traditions and in our memory of the past, features numerous enough to justify the vindication of the Unity of Negro Culture.

That is why the second Conference means:

1) To express our specific problems and deal with mankind's major problems in our works by drawing on our peoples for our sources of inspirations and our resources of expression.
2) to build up a community of cultural "totems."
3) to build up a community of evidences.
4) to build up a community of style and expression.

The agenda we propose comprises two parts:

1) The foundation of our culture and its chances of achieving unity and solidarity.
2) The tasks and the responsibilities of each discipline or art.

The first part will be the topic of three studies (on the past, the present and the future of our culture) confided to three specialists or groups of specialists.

The second part will comprise a series of studies on the present tasks and responsibilities of the historian, the linguist, the theologian, the scientist, the poet, etc. . . . (bearing always in mind our preoccupation with solidarity).

Finally, a closing resolution or motion is envisaged which, from what precedes, will aim at bringing out the main points of our cultural policy.

— Reading No. 21 —

JOMO KENYATTA BETWEEN TWO WORLDS *

Author of the widely read Tell Freedom *and other novels, Peter Abrahams is one of Africa's leading novelists. Having left his South African home, he has traveled over Africa, England, and the United States and now lives in Jamaica. In this article, Abrahams describes the renewal of his friendship with Jomo Kenyatta, now Kenya's Prime Minister, whom he had known in England.*

↱   ↱   ↱

He took me to his home. It was a big, sprawling, empty place on the brow of a hill. Inside, it had nothing to make for comfort. There were hard wooden chairs, a few tables and only the bed in the bedroom. There were no books, none of the normal amenities of western civilization. When we arrived two women emerged from somewhere in the back and hovered about in the shadows. They brought in liquor, but I never got a clear glimpse of either of them. My friend's anguish of spirit was such that I did not want to ask questions. We sat on the veranda and drank steadily and in silence until we were both miserably, depressingly drunk.

And then Kenyatta began to speak in a low, bitter voice of his frustration and of the isolated position in which he found himself. He had no friends. There was no one in the tribe who could give him the intellectual companionship that had become so important to him in his years in Europe. The things that were important to him—consequential conversation, the drink that represented a social activity rather than the intention to get drunk, the concept of individualism, the inviolability of privacy—all these were alien to the tribesmen in whose midst he lived. So Kenyatta, the western man, was driven in on himself and was forced to assert himself in tribal terms. Only thus would the tribesmen follow him and so give him his position of power and importance as a leader.

To live without roots is to live in hell, and no man chooses voluntarily to live in hell. The people who could answer his

needs as a western man had erected a barrier of color against
him in spite of the fact that the taproots of their culture had
become the taproots of his culture too. By denying him access
to those things which complete the life of western man, they
had forced him back into the tribalism from which he had
so painfully freed himself over the years.

None of this was stated explicitly by either Kenyatta or
myself. But it was there in his brooding bitter commentary
on both the tribes and the white settlers of the land. For me,
Kenyatta became that night a man who in his own life per-
sonified the terrible tragedy of Africa and the terrible secret
war that rages in it. He was the victim both of tribalism and
of westernism gone sick. His heart and mind and body were
the battlefield of the ugly violence known as the Mau Mau
revolt long before it broke out in that beautiful land. The
tragedy is that he was so rarely gifted, that he could have
made such a magnificent contribution in other circumstances.

— Reading No. 22 —

YOUNG AFRICA'S RESOLVE

*In the following two poems, Dennis Osadebay, Premier of
the Mid-Western Region of Nigeria, evinces the yearning for
knowledge of the outside world that permeates the African
intellectual class; there is no fear of the loss of African customs in "Young Africa's Plea."*

✓   ✓   ✓

Young Africa's Resolve*

I'll talk no more,
I'll listen to nobody's talk,

I'll wait no more;
I'll lead myself towards the goal,
Though countless hurdles cross my path
And danger lurks on every side,
I'll go forward and do and dare.

* *An Anthology of West African Verse,* compiled by Olembe
   Bassir (Ibadan: Ibadan University Press, 1957), p. 52.

On library doors
I'll knock aloud and gain entrance;
Of the strength
Of nations past and present I will read,
I'll brush the dust from ancient scrolls,
And drinking deep of the Pyrrhean stream,
Will go forward and do and dare.

I'll sail the seas
And learn the might of God and man
Behind my name
To tie a string of alphabets,
Melting bubbles, will not end all.
I'll come back home with strong arms bared,
I'll go forward and do and dare.

Young Africa's Plea*

Don't preserve my customs
As some fine curios
To suit some white historian's tastes.
There's nothing artificial
That beats the natural way,
In culture and ideals of life.
Let me play with the white man's ways,
Let me work with the black man's brains,
Let my affairs themselves sort out.
Then in sweet re-birth
I'll rise a better man,
Not ashamed to face the world.
Those who doubt my talents
In secret fear my strength;
They know I am no less a man.
Let them bury their prejudice,
Let them show their noble sides,
Let me have untrammelled growth.
My friends will never know regret
And I, I never once forget.

* *An Anthology of West African Verse,* compiled by Olembe
  Bassir (Ibadan: Ibadan University Press, 1957), p. 57.

NKRUMAH ON THE NEED FOR PAN-AFRICANISM, 1960*

Excerpts from this address to the Ghana National Assembly by President Kwame Nkrumah on August 8, 1960, must be understood in the setting of the turmoil in the Congo created by the presence of Belgian troops and the secession of Katanga. Nkrumah reiterates his appeal for African political unity.

. . . The African struggle for independence and unity must begin with political union. A loose confederation of economic cooperation is deceptively time-delaying. It is only a political union that will ensure a uniformity in our foreign policy projecting the African personality and presenting Africa as a force important to be reckoned with. I repeat, a loose economic co-operation means a screen behind which detractors, imperialist and colonialist protagonists and African puppet leaders hide to operate and weaken the concept of any effort to realise African unity and independence. A political union envisages a common foreign and defence policy, and rapid social, economic and industrial developments. The economic resources of Africa are immense and staggering. It is only by unity that these resources can be utilised for the progress of the Continent and for the happiness of mankind.

We must learn from history. The genius of the South American people has been to a considerable extent frustrated by the fact that when the Spanish and Portuguese colonial empires dissolved they did not organise themselves into a United States of South America. At the same time, when South America became free, the colonial States which acquired their independence were potentially as powerful as the United States in North America. Their failure to come together resulted in one part of the American continent developing at the expense of the other. Nevertheless, there is only one country in South America, namely Paraguay, which has a population of less than three million.

* *An Anthology of West African Verse,* compiled by Olembe 1960).

At the moment independent States in Africa are being established with populations of less than a million. Territories in Africa which have become independent or are likely to become independent in the near future, and which have populations of less than three million, include the Central African Republic, Chad, the former French Congo (which has a population of only three-quarters of a million) Dahomey, Gabon with a population of less than half a million, the Ivory Coast, Niger, Sierra Leone and Togoland.

It is impossible to imagine that the colonial powers seriously believe that independence could be of much value to these African States in such a terrible state of fragmentation. Surely this is only in pursuance of the old policy of divide and rule. Colonialism invented the system of indirect rule. The essence of this system was that a chief appeared nominally in control while actually he was manipulated from behind the scenes by the colonial power. The setting up of States of this nature appears to be only a logical development of the discredited theory of indirect rule. . . .

There is a real danger that the colonial powers will grant a nominal type of political independence to individual small units so as to ensure that the same old colonial type of economic organisation continues long after independence has been achieved. This in itself is a source of the gravest potential danger for the whole world. The peoples of Africa do not seek political freedom for abstract purposes. They seek it because they believe that through political freedom they can obtain economic advancement, education and a real control over their own destiny. If there is a grant of independence to a State which is so small that it cannot mobilise its own resources and which is tied by a series of economic and military agreements to the former colonial power, then a potentially revolutionary situation is at once created. These are the situations facing the new Africa of today. . . .

DECLARATION OF THE ALL-AFRICAN PEOPLES' CONFERENCE, 1959*

The All-African Peoples' Conference was formed to link nationalist movements in those areas not yet independent with those that were. This Declaration of 1959 forcefully expresses its aim. Since then, Nyasaland, Northern Rhodesia, the Congo, and Algeria have secured self-government, and the only remaining areas of European control are the Portuguese territories, Southern Rhodesia, the High Commission Territories, and the Union of South Africa.

✓   ✓   ✓

(1) In response to the urgent appeal of African nationalist leaders of Nyasaland, the Rhodesias and the Belgian Congo for aid and assistance against the brutal offensive of the forces of imperialism and colonialism let loose on the peoples in these territories, and conscious of our responsibility to our fellow African Freedom Fighters, the Steering Committee of the All-African Peoples' Conference convened a special Emergency Meeting in Conakry, Guinea, on 15th April 1959, the first anniversary of African Freedom Day.

(2) Shocked and horrified by the reports of the accredited representatives of the Nyasaland National Congress, the S.R. National Congress, the Mouvement National Congolais, the Congolese Democratic Party (Abako) and the Cameroons Progressive Union, this meeting declares its solidarity with our brothers and comrades imprisoned or exiled and demands their immediate release. We also sent a message of sympathy to the relatives of the unarmed and defenceless men and women killed for no other crime than supporting by non-violent means the demand for racial equality, human dignity and national independence. . . .

* Kanyama Chiume, *Nyasaland Demands Secession and Independence: An Appeal to Africa* (London: The Twentieth Century Press, 1959), pp. 24-25.

(4) We appeal to the independent African States, to our brothers in Asia, to Africans and peoples of African descent, to the religious leaders of the world and to all true friends and champions of African Freedom to join with us in condemning the wanton brutality of the authorities in the Federation of Central Africa, especially in Nyasaland and the Belgian Congo, and to render every assistance—financial and moral—to relieve the sufferings of those in distress of our brothers in these territories.

(5) In conformity to the Charter of the United Nations and the Universal Declaration of Human Rights, we request the members of the United Nations to make a clear and unequivocal declaration whether or not they unconditionally support the legitimate aspirations of the African Freedom Fighters for self-determination and independence. Those who are not with us in this hour of crisis shall not only be considered the enemies of the colonial peoples of Africa, but the independent African States as well. For, as the resolution of the Accra Conference warns, as long as there remains one imperialist stronghold on this African Continent, the freedom and security of every independent African State is faced with the danger of aggression.

(6) The situation demands our constant watchfulness and vigilance. All imperialist intrigues, manoeuvres and acts of subversion aimed at discrediting the independent African States and undermining their tranquility and security must be unmasked and exposed as part of a consorted plan by the colonialist powers to keep Africa divided and weak.

(7) Not unmindful of the tragic events in Algeria where our comrades are defending themselves against the armed violence of French imperialism, this Emergency Meeting of the Steering Committee of the A.A.P.C. therefore calls upon all workers by hand and brain, all tillers of the soil, all progressive and patriotic intellectuals, the women and youths of Africa, to close their ranks, unite their forces and discipline themselves for the final liquidation of colonialism and racialism by means of non-violence, non-co-operation, i.e., the strike economic boycott wherever necessary and possible.

(8) We categorically reject the claim of those imperialists who assert that Africa is a part or continuation of Europe, and we denounce and repudiate those African misleaders who would have our Continent continue to be misruled from London, Paris, Brussels, Lisbon or Madrid, under any guise or form. We proclaim and support the African Personality within the African Community.

Forward to independence now!
Long live the unbreakable unity of the African peoples!
Long live the All-African Peoples' Conference!

— Reading No. 25 —

"ZIK" ON PAN-AFRICANISM, 1959*

*In an address in London on July 31, 1959, the then Premier
of the Eastern Region and President of the National Council
of Nigeria and the Cameroons (later President of Nigeria),
Dr. Nnamdi Azikiwe, explained his attitude on the manner
of African unification. Zik's approach differed from Nkrumah's.*

I believe that economic and social integration will enable
Nigeria and its neighbors to bring to pass the United States
of Africa, which is the dream of African nationalists. It
would be capital folly to assume that hard-bargaining politicians who passed through the ordeal of victimization and
the crucible of persecution to win their political independence
will easily surrender their newly-won political power in the
interest of a political leviathan which is populated by people
who are alien to one another in their social and economic
relations. It has not been possible in Europe or America.
. . . I reiterate that I firmly believe in the attainment of an
association or union of African States either on a regional or
continental basis in the future. I would regard such a future
as not within the life-time of the heroes and heroines who
have spearheaded the struggle for freedom in Africa, these
four decades. . . . In other words, the *prerequisites of political integration in Africa are the economic and social integration of African peoples . . . [italics added].*

* Dr. Nnamdi Azikiwe, *Zik: Selected Speeches of Dr. Nnamdi
    Azikiwe* (Cambridge: Cambridge University Press,
    1961), p. 72.

CASABLANCA v. MONROVIA, 1962 *

The rift between the Casablanca and Monrovia blocs was not only over the different paths to African unity, but also over foreign and economic policy. The following brief description of the Casablanca view was written at the time of the Lagos conference of the Monrovian powers in January 1962. It is pro-Casablanca.

✦ ✦ ✦

The unfortunate split in the trends of independent African States marked by the absence of the foreign ministers of Morocco, Ghana, Guinea, Mali and the United Arab Republic from the Lagos Conference and by the withdrawal of the Sudan from that Conference, is just what the Western powers, or at least some of them, want.

The Foreign Ministers of the five absent countries had met in Accra during the past week. One of the reasons why they had declined the invitation of the Monrovia Conference members to attend the Lagos Conference, was the fact that the Algerian Provisional Government had not been invited. . . .

Difficulty

The Foreign Ministers in Lagos were supposed to prepare a 'Summit' meeting of the participating countries. The schedule and all necessary arrangements for the Lagos meeting had been prepared by the member states of the Monrovia Conference without consulting the Casablanca countries. This was another factor which made it difficult for the Casablanca Powers to attend.

Furthermore, even if Morocco's grievance that Mauretania, which forms part of her sovereign territory, had been invited to Lagos as a separate state, had not been cited among the reasons which prevented the Casablanca countries from going to Lagos, it would have proved to be a stumbling block anyhow.

* *The Party*, No. 19, 16-28 February 1962 (Accra: Convention People's Party Bureau of Information and Publicity), p. 11.

As it turned out these minor difficulties could have been solved; the Casablanca countries showed their willingness to meet the Monrovia members in order to prevent dissension among the African peoples:

Even if we disregard the question of Algeria's invitation and Morocco's grievance, there remains a more serious basic difference between the lines of policy of the two groups both on the international and home levels. While the Casablanca Six pledged themselves to pursue a policy of non-alignment in order to preserve their hard-won independence, their sovereignty, their territorial integrity, and to contribute to the strengthening of world peace, the Monrovia group consists of countries which were practically all under colonialist influence. The Members of the French Community, who form a sizeable bloc, are all autonomous states but adopt a definitely French, not say a Western, line of policy.

Economically, the Casablanca Six have established their economic independence and are exploiting their national wealth for the benefit of their masses while the members of the French Community as well as many of the former British colonies continue to be exploited by their former colonialist masters. Their people still toil in poverty while Europe saps their wealth. . . .

Non-Alignment

The joint communique issued in Accra declared that the Casablanca Powers aim at closer co-operation on a larger scale politically and economically with all African countries on the basis of independence. The words on the basis of independence are not without significance. The Casablanca Powers rightly consider that the Monrovia group is dominated by the Western powers. They also suspect the nature of the Lagos conference and fear that some foreign powers may exploit it for splitting the African Continent into two groups with one group serving as an instrument for fighting non-alignment.

BIBLIOGRAPHY

Abraham, W. E., *The Mind of Africa* (Chicago: University of Chicago, 1963)

Amamoo, J. G., *The New Ghana* (London: Pan Books Ltd., 1958)

Apter, David E., *Ghana in Transition* (New York: Atheneum, 1963)

Awolowo, Obafemi, *Path to Nigerian Freedom* (London: Faber and Faber Ltd., 1947)

Awolowo, Chief Obafemi, *Awo: Autobiography* (Cambridge: Cambridge University Press, 1960)

Azikiwe, Nnamdi, *Zik: A Selection of Speeches* (Cambridge: Cambridge University Press, 1961)

Bassir, Olumbe, editor, *An Anthology of West African Verse* (Ibadan: Ibadan University Press, 1957)

Buell, Raymond L., *The Native Problem in Africa*, 2 vols. (New York: The Macmillan Co., 1928)

Carter, Gwendolen, *The Politics of Inequality: South Africa Since 1948* (London: Thames and Hudson, 1959)

Carter, Gwendolen, *Independence for Africa* (New York: Frederick A. Praeger, 1960)

Coleman, James S., *Nigeria: Background to Nationalism* (Berkeley: University of California Press, 1960)

Cronon, Edmund D., *Black Moses: The Story of Marcus Garvey* (Madison: The University of Wisconsin Press, 1955)

Deuxieme Congres des Ecrivains et Artistes Noirs, 2 vols. (Paris: Presence Africaine, 1959)

Dia, Mamadou, *The African Nations and World Solidarity* (New York: Frederick A. Praeger, 1961)

DuBois, W. E. Burghardt, *The World and Africa* (New York: The Viking Press, 1947)

Duffy, James, and Manners, Robert A., *Africa Speaks* (Princeton: D. Van Nostrand Company, Inc., 1961)

Epelle, Sam, *The Promise of Nigeria* (London: Pan Books, Ltd., 1960)

Feit, Edward, *South Africa: The Dynamics of the African*

National Congress (London: Oxford University Press, 1962)

The First International Conference of Negro Writers and Artists (Paris: Presence Africaine, 1956)

Hodgkin, Thomas, *Nationalism in Colonial Africa* (New York: New York University Press, 1957)

Hodgkin, Thomas, *African Political Parties* (Baltimore: Penguin Books, 1961)

Hughes, Langston, editor, *An African Treasury* (New York: Pyramid Books, 1961)

Judd, Peter, editor, *African Independence* (New York: Dell Publishing Co., 1962)

Jahn, Janheinz, *Muntu: The New African Culture* (New York: Grove Press, Inc., 1961)

Kenyatta, Jomo, *Facing Mt. Kenya* (New York: Vintage Books, 1962)

Kuper, Leo, *Passive Resistance in South Africa* (New Haven: Yale University Press, 1957)

Legum, Colin, *Pan-Africanism* (New York: Frederick A. Praeger, 1962)

Mphahlele, Ezekiel, *The African Image* (New York: Frederick A. Praeger, 1962)

Mboya, Tom, *Freedom and After* (Boston: Little, Brown & Co., 1963)

Nkrumah, Kwame, *Ghana* (Edinburgh: Thomas Nelson and Sons, Ltd., 1959)

Nkrumah, Kwame, *I Speak of Freedom* (New York: Frederick A. Praeger, 1961)

Nkrumah, Kwame, *Africa Must Unite* (New York: Frederick A. Praeger, 1963)

Oliver, Roland, and Fage, J. D., *A Short History of Africa* (Baltimore: Penguin Books, 1962)

Padmore, George, *Pan-Africanism or Communism?* (New York: Roy Publishers, 1956)

Quaison-Sackey, Alex, *Africa Unbound* (New York: Frederick A. Praeger, 1963)

Rutherford, Peggy, editor, *African Voices* (New York: Grosset & Dunlap, 1958)

Segal, Ronald, *Political Africa: A Who's Who of Personalities and Parties* (New York: Frederick A. Praeger, 1961)

Senghor, Leopold S., *African Socialism* (New York: The American Society of African Culture, 1959)

Shepherd, George W., Jr., *The Politics of African Nationalism* (New York: Frederick A. Praeger, 1962)

Sithole, Ndabaningi, *African Nationalism* (Cape Town: Oxford University Press, 1959)

Tempels, Rev. Placide, *Bantu Philosophy* (Paris: Presence Africaine, 1959)

Van Rensburg, Patrick, *Guilty Land: The History of Apartheid* (New York: Frederick A. Praeger, 1962)

Periodicals

Africa Digest, London
Africa Report, Washington, D. C.
Africa, South In Exile, London (ceased publication)
Africa Today, New York
African Affairs, London
African Studies Bulletin, New York
AMSAC Newsletter, New York
Black Orpheus, Ibadan
Journal of African History, London
The Journal of Modern African Studies, London
Présence Africaine, Paris

AFRICAN NATIONALISM:
A SELECTED CHRONOLOGY

——	Mediaeval African kingdoms
1844	Bond, English protection of Fantis
1871	Fanti Confederation
1892	Ethiopian Church, South Africa
1897	Aborigines' Rights Protection Society
1912	South African Native National Congress
1913	Above changed to African National Congress
1914	Federation of Nigeria
1915	Chilembwe Uprising, Shire Highlands
1919	First Pan-African Congress, Paris
1920	Marcus Garvey's Universal Negro Improvement Association
1920	West African National Congress
1920	Industrial and Commercial Workers' Union (I.C.U.), South Africa
1921	Second Pan-African Congress
1922	Egyptian Independence
1922	Nigerian National Democratic Party

1922	Kikuyu Central Association (K.C.A.), Kenya
1923	Clifford Constitution, Nigeria
1923	Third Pan-African Congress
1925	West African Students' Union, London
1927	Fourth Pan-African Congress
1935	Italian invasion of Ethiopia
1935	All-African Convention, South Africa
1936	"Natives" suffrage withdrawn, South Africa
1936	Nigerian Youth Movement
1937	International African Service Bureau
1937-38	Cocoa "hold-up," Gold Coast
1938	National Youth Charter, Nigeria
1941	Atlantic Charter
1944	Brazzaville conference on post-war French Africa
1944	National Council of Nigeria and the Cameroons (NCNC)
1945	Fifth Pan-African Congress, Manchester
1945	General strike, Nigeria
1946	Kenya African Union (KAU)
1947	United Gold Coast Convention
1948	Gold Coast riots
1949	African National Congress' Programme of Action, South Africa
1949	Convention People's Party (CPP), Gold Coast
1950	Positive Action campaign, Gold Coast
1952	Libyan Independence
1952-60	Mau Mau, Kenya
1952-53	Defiance Campaign, South Africa
1954-62	Algerian war
1954	Lyttelton federal constitution, Nigeria
1955	Afro-Asian Conference, Bandung
1955	"Freedom Charter," South Africa
1955	Sudan proclaims its independence
1956	"Loi cadre," French African territories
1956	Independence of Tunisia
1956	First International Congress of Negro Writers and Artists, Paris
1956	Independence of Morocco
1957	Society for African Culture
1957	Independence of Ghana
1958	Independence of Guinea
1958	First Conference of Independent African States, Accra
1958	All-African People's Conference, Accra
1959	Second International Congress of Negro Writers and Artists, Rome
1959	Pan Africanist Congress, South Africa

1960	Year of independence for Cameroun, Togo, Mali, Senegal, Malagasy, Congo Republic (Belgian), Somalia (Italian and British), Dahomey, Niger, Upper Volta, Ivory Coast, Chad, Central African Republic, Congo Republic (French), Gabon, Nigeria, Mauretania
1960	Sharpeville killings, South Africa
1960	African Nationalist Congress and Pan Africanist Congress banned, South Africa
1960	Second Conference of Independent African States
1960	Ghana becomes a Republic
1960	Mali split into Senegal and Mali
1960	Brazzaville bloc
1961	Casablanca bloc
1961	Murder of Patrice Lumumba, Congo
1961	All-African Trade Union Federation
1961-3	Mali-Guinea-Ghana Union
1961	Monrovia bloc
1961	Independence of Sierra Leone
1961	Independence of Tanganyika
1962	Pan African Freedom Movement of East and Central Africa broadens membership to include southern Africa (PAFMECSA)
1962	First International Congress of Africanists, Accra
1962	Inter-African and Malagasy Organization, Lagos
1962	Independence of Ruanda and Burundi
1962	Independence of Algeria
1962	Independence of Uganda
1962-63	Katangan secession ended, Congo
1962-63	Awolowo treason trial, Nigeria
1963	Organization of African Unity (OAU), Addis Ababa (Most important organization for African unity to date)
1963	Beginnings of Transkei "self-government" (apartheid)
1963	Nigeria becomes a Republic
1963	Independence of Kenya
1963	Central African Federation (Southern and Northern Rhodesia and Nyasaland) dissolved
1964	Independence of Malawi (Nyasaland)
1964	Independence of Zambia (Northern Rhodesia)
1964	Union of Tanganyika and Zanzibar (Tanzania)
1964	Civil war in the Congo

INDEX

191

About this Book:

African nationalism was once dismissed as a pastime of the intellectual elite. Today, it is on the march on the whole continent; and is conceived of as the necessary framework for, and the propelling force behind, catapulting Africa into this turbulent twentieth century. In this volume, the original narrative surveys the historical backgrounds and political loyalties, policies, and situations of the diverse countries of this continent. It also examines the African personality and *négritude,* and various Pan-African movements. The twenty-six informative documents cover a wide range of political events, and sketch some of the leading figures involved in the African national movement—Kenyatta, Lumumba, and Nkrumah.

VAN NOSTRAND ANVIL BOOKS

ANVIL BOOKS, under the general editorship of Louis L. Snyder, make a unique and valuable contribution to the fields of history and the social sciences. In each title a distinguished scholar offers an original analysis of a major problem area, incorporating the most recent research. For ready reference to source materials, each book includes a selection of pertinent documents, many from neglected or hard-to-find sources. Brief, handy and readable, each book is priced at $1.45. A complete listing of the ANVIL BOOKS now available appears on the final page of this book.

LOUIS L. SNYDER, general editor of ANVIL BOOKS, is Professor of History at the City College of New York, where he has been teaching since 1933. A graduate of St. John's College (Maryland), he received his doctorate from the University of Frankfurt-am-Main, Germany, in 1931. Dr. Snyder has written or edited numerous books, including *The Dynamics of Nationalism* and *The Imperialism Reader* (Van Nostrand); *The War: A Concise History, 1939-1945,* available in British, Japanese, Danish, Swedish, and Dutch editions; *A Survey of European Civilization* (2 vols.); *The Meaning of Nationalism;* and *German Nationalism.* He was the co-editor of the best-seller, *A Treasury of Great Reporting.*

8395

D. VAN NOSTRAND COMPANY, Inc.
120 Alexander Street   Princeton, N. J.